THE WELLS OF SALVATION

THE WELLS OF SALVATION

With joy shall ye draw water
out of the wells of salvation
ISAIAH 12:3

A SERIES OF SEVEN ADDRESSES
GIVEN BY
JOHN METCALFE

THE PUBLISHING TRUST
Church Road, Tylers Green, Penn, Buckinghamshire.

Printed and Published by
John Metcalfe Publishing Trust
Church Road, Tylers Green
Penn, Buckinghamshire

—

Distributed by Trust Representatives
and Agents world-wide

In the Far East

Bethany, Orchard Point P.O. Box 0373
Singapore 912313

—

—

First Published 1975
Reprinted 1980
Second Edition 1997

—

ISBN 1 870039 72 6. 2nd edition
(ISBN 0 9502515 6 9. 1st edition)

—

CONTENTS

THE FIRST ADDRESS

THE WELLS OF SALVATION

The First Address

And in that day thou shalt say, O LORD, I will praise thee: though thou wast angry with me, thine anger is turned away, and thou comfortedst me. Behold, God is my salvation; I will trust, and not be afraid: for the LORD JEHOVAH is my strength and my song; he also is become my salvation. Therefore with joy shall ye draw water out of the wells of salvation.

Isaiah 12:1-3.

1. Isaiah's Prophetic Ministry

THERE is no question that out of all the old testament Isaiah must be the choice evangelical prophet. The predictions in Isaiah of the divine Person, of the humanity, the birth, the temptations, the travails, the ministry, and finally of the death and resurrection of Christ: all of these future events are as clearly foreseen by the prophet, as is the image of heights above and beyond reflected in the tranquil waters of a still pool in the foothills below and before.

Likewise the prophet's foretelling of Christ having ascended, of his receiving and giving the Spirit, of his seeing of the travail of his soul and being satisfied. The universal spread of the gospel also, with the conversion of the Gentiles, even unto the remotest isles that waited for his law: all of these truths are transparently mirrored in and reflected by the book of Isaiah the prophet.

So it is with the seer's insight into the heavenly ministry of Christ from on high and his view of the spiritual inworking of the Holy Ghost here below: this is pure divinity. His visionary portrayal of the raising up of the church through the preaching of the gospel, the prophet's precognition of the vital experiences of real Christians, his discernment of the evangelical ministration of the Spirit: all this was as if Isaiah had sat in the counsels of the Godhead discerning the determination of eternal purpose from within the omniscience of the Deity.

In the volume of the book the old covenant is acutely distinguished from the new, the law separated from the gospel, so that Isaiah shines like a beacon, beaming out the light of grace. He declares the terms of the new testament; we find election, predestination, justification, and adoption mightily established in the context of the sovereignty of God, and more strongly represented in Isaiah's prophecy than in any other.

The new testament is brought out in so singular a manner, emphasizing the connection between the way of faith and the revelation of the deity of Christ and Christ's offices. His kingly government, his prophetic doctrine, his expiatory sufferings, his priestly ministrations: all are here even more poignantly displayed than in many of the new testament books.

Indeed the latter, written some one thousand years after the book of the prophet Isaiah—and in which history is recorded in retrospect, not foretold in prophecy—are in some ways less vivid and panoramic than that which Isaiah wrote by the Spirit so many long centuries before even the advent of Christ.

Hence it is that one discovers Isaiah's prophetic foresight at times to be more penetrating, more eagle-eyed, than the divine historians' memorial hindsight. And not only in doctrine, but sensation also. The experiences of the soul-travail of awakened sinners, of the way in which God brings a sinner to Christ, of the inward impressions created by the foreclosures of a frowning providence, the manifold variety of interior sensations experienced through the sanctification of the Spirit within the soul: how wonderfully does the prophet expound them.

Scanning the firmament Isaiah descries the priestly ministry of Christ, ascended above all heavens. From on high the Son intercedes for those whom the Father draws to himself. The evangelical prophet further declares the inward trials, doubts, fears, and spiritual anguish of the elect; of each stage of interior progress. This whilst as yet they know not the Lord and feel they never will know him—and yet cannot but seek him—of all these things Isaiah speaks most pathetically and sympathetically.

Isaiah's prophecy speaks of penitent sinners' reception into covenant favour. Of their justification in the Lord their righteousness. Of their holding to the heavenly vision and persevering towards the country that is very far off, gaining sweet glimpses of the heavenly city and beholding the King there in his beauty.

The prophet predicts of the coming of the Lord to judgment, the end of the world, of the resurrection from the dead, of the torments of the damned and the glories of the just. Of all these things Isaiah treats in what has been called 'The gospel according to Isaiah', and that because the great evangelical penetration and prophetic insight of the seer spread before the reader the wondrous ministry of Christ in the new testament, virtually a whole millennium before the coming of the Son of God into the world.

In the chapter before the one under consideration, the prophet declares in a figure the way in which Christ should appear to them that look for him. He is viewed as a root out of a dry ground. This green shoot is seen as obtaining moisture where none appears: as springing out of a barren desert. Christ is depicted as a moist, rich, sap-filled, green branch. 'There shall come forth a rod out of the stem of Jesse, and a Branch shall grow out of his roots', Isaiah 11:1.

And of his ministry it is said, 'The spirit of the LORD shall rest upon him, the spirit of wisdom and understanding, the spirit of counsel and might, the spirit of knowledge and of the fear of the LORD.' This is speaking of the Lord's humanity, for the going forth of the Son of man is well portrayed in Isaiah. The prophet is so favoured with perception that he discerns betimes the ministry of Christ clearer than the very apostles were able to perceive it, even at that time when they actually walked with Jesus in the flesh through the land of Israel at the beginning of the gospel.

The prophet already mirrors the service of Christ in that ministry which comes from his being ascended up on high, when, as a result of travail, suffering, and death for his people in the world, Christ now ascends to God and the Father and is given and receives for his purchased people the gift of the Holy Ghost. It is by that invisible Spirit that the Son of God is seen as exercising his ministry on earth from so elevated a place in heaven. This is Isaiah's view of the ministry of Christ.

And yet the very apostles themselves thought—when Christ was dead and buried—that it had all come to nothing; it was finished; their dream ended; 'I go a fishing'. 'We trusted that it had been he which should have redeemed Israel.' Until they actually experienced—what Isaiah never experienced—the gift of the Holy Ghost on the day of Pentecost, they downright refused to apply to Jesus what had been believed and spoken of him some one thousand years before. 'O fools, and slow of heart to believe all that the prophets have spoken', Luke 24:25.

So I would bring before you that Isaiah singularly displays to us the truth of the new testament, and nowhere more so than when he writes in Isaiah 12:3, 'Therefore with joy shall ye draw water out of the wells of salvation'.

Now let us consider this and enquire how water is drawn from the wells of salvation. No earthly wells these: they are wells of salvation. No natural water is in them, for water drawn from the wells of salvation is altogether different from that worldly water drawn to slake bodily thirst on a burning day in a dry and parched land.

Water from the wells of salvation is spiritual and another thing than that drawn from earthly wells such as the well that Jacob gave to Israel. Here Jesus said to the woman of Samaria, 'If thou knewest the gift of God, and who it is that saith to thee, Give me to drink; thou wouldest have asked of him, and he would have given thee living water.' For he had asked her to give him to drink of that natural water which stood in Jacob's well in the dusty ground, and she taunted him and said, 'How is it that thou, being a Jew, askest drink of me, which am a woman of Samaria?'.

But his request for a drink of natural water to slake earthly thirst that will come again was nothing compared to her need for living water from the well of salvation, which if a man drink he shall never thirst again: for it is in him a well springing up unto everlasting life. And this is that of which our verse in Isaiah speaks: water from the wells of salvation. For everyone knows that after drinking water from any natural well the thirst returns within a few hours, and if it is really hot within a few minutes; but Christ speaketh of another water, from other wells, namely water from the wells of salvation, which answers not to bodily thirst but to soul thirst.

That water which Christ gives answers therefore not to material, physical water for bodily craving, but to that which slakes and internally satisfies the longing soul in respect of things spiritual, of interior religion, of thirst for salvation, of craving for the living God. The water which Christ gives is such that, If a man drink of it he shall never thirst again. Now of this water evidently some must drink, for it is spoken of them in Isaiah 12:3, 'Therefore with joy shall ye draw water out of the wells of salvation'. And this is my enquiry, Who are they, and how do they do so?

2. The Premise regarding the Wells of Salvation: 'Therefore'

First observe, What precedes the drawing of water

Notice the first word of our text. It is THEREFORE. Therefore with joy shall ye draw water out of the wells of salvation. 'Therefore' refers the reader to that which is the premise of water being drawn from the wells of salvation. There is a prior condition, a previous requirement, before water can be drawn. Water may not be drawn irrespectively, because in fact something must be precedent for the wells to be forthcoming.

Hence the word 'therefore'—meaning, on account of that which precedes—points back to the cause of which the drawn water is the effect. It is on account of that which went before, that water presently is to be drawn. 'Therefore' indicates the foundation upon which water is obtained from Christ to satisfy thirsty souls. The ground is indicated in this word 'therefore' and it is put there to show that drawing spiritual water can only be on this basis, namely that indicated in the previous two verses; *that* is why water is drawn. *Therefore* ye shall draw water.

Let us observe these verses then, because only on account of what they describe can such drawing be effectual: 'And in that day thou shalt say, O LORD, I will praise thee: though thou wast angry with me, thine anger is turned away, and thou comfortedst me. Behold, God is my salvation; I will trust, and not be afraid: for the LORD JEHOVAH is my strength and my song; he also is become my salvation. *Therefore* with joy shall ye draw water out of the wells of salvation.'

So you see that one cannot just draw water from the wells irrespective of prior spiritual experience. The drawing is consequential. Neither does the verse encourage the sons and daughters of men indiscriminately and promiscuously to hope to draw water, for the cause and origin preceding its being drawn must be discovered to oneself personally.

As Christ said to the woman, 'If thou knewest the gift of God, and who it is that saith to thee, Give me to drink; thou wouldest have asked of him, and he would have given thee living water.' If she had known the gift of God, do you see? You have got to find *him* first. Says Christ, you would have said to *me*, 'Give me to drink'. You see that one must know the Son of God—who is himself the gift of God—in order to get water out of the wells of salvation. The Father must first reveal the Son.

Hence, I say, it is absolutely useless indiscriminately to advise men and women to hope for water from the wells of salvation unless GOD has become their salvation. If God has become their salvation, then they shall draw water out of the wells of salvation. GOD must be apprehended spiritually before water can be drawn which satisfies soul-thirst and makes the helpless cravings, the restless gaspings, the dry pantings, and the unintelligible longings that are locked within the breast of men and women, coherent and meaningful.

How dreadful is this soul-thirst! 'As the hart panteth after the water brooks, so panteth my soul after thee, O God.' This is far worse than the maddening craving for water in the desert when with cracked and blackened lips the lost soul reels, totters, and cries out for water. Dreadful as is this natural state, the spiritual is worse. Yet for all this the thirsty soul must *first* find GOD as Saviour in order that in consequence water may then be drawn from the wells of salvation.

So I would bring this before you, that drawing water out of the wells of salvation is an indirect matter, not a direct one. The knowledge of GOD as Saviour is precedent to drawing water. Hence I take this word 'Therefore', and I enquire, What is it to have GOD as one's Saviour? 'Behold, God is my salvation.' Now it is not that God is the church's salvation. This is personal, this is inward. It precedes the church and is the cause of one's being of the church. It is not that salvation is deposited in the church and is automatically applicable to the external members thereof, no, not at all.

This is something that no church, nothing, and nobody else can obtain for one. This is something God does for one personally and here is the soul saying: 'GOD is *my* salvation, *I* will trust, and not be afraid: for the LORD JEHOVAH is *my* strength and *my* song; he also is become *my* salvation.' That is this soul's experience, and experience in the first person, and that is why he can draw water from the wells of salvation in consequence. The word 'therefore' indicates a state of salvation. But the salvation with which this soul is saved is qualified, it is being saved by GOD.

You might think that being saved needs no qualification, but it does, especially today. Indeed, it is popular now to drop the words 'saved' and 'salvation'. They are regarded as being rather old-fashioned, somewhat out of date, amongst those confusing archaic authorized Olde English words hard to be understood. They should be liberated from the harsh rigidity of translating what it says, into the gentle softness of saying what we mean.

What is preferred today is rather along the line of: 'I have committed my life to God.' So that you are asked whether you are 'a committed Christian'—the assumption being that all are

Christians in any event, by birth from 'Christian' parents, and it is just a question of 'committal' later in life.

A greater deception and contrariety against the truth cannot be imagined. How then could God subsequently *become* my salvation? For if I am born a Christian or else am one from infancy by a few drops of water then God must have been my salvation in the first instance. But it does not say Christendom has become one's salvation. And in truth it is not a matter either of environment or of what one does, much less of what the church does to one: it is what GOD does that matters in salvation.

Neither does 'God is become my salvation' equate with 'giving your heart to Jesus'. For the man that really knows his heart learns 'out of the heart proceed evil thoughts, murders, adulteries, fornications, thefts, false witness, blasphemies'—a suited gift for men to offer to God?

The awakened sinner becomes aware that the heart is deceitful above all things and desperately wicked, and the truth is, he despairs of salvation because he cannot offer such a filthy heart. Give it to Jesus? What conceit makes men imagine either that this is any kind of a gift to offer, or that he is obliged to accept so foul, so vile a 'gift'?

Indeed, have they never read that 'God gave them up to uncleanness through the lusts of their own hearts'? Give them back, then? Let Jesus into *that*, then? Salvation is not 'giving one's heart'. It is God giving one 'a new heart', and, 'a new spirit will I put within you'. Indeed, the man that really knows his heart despairs of it and himself and cries, 'I can of mine own self do nothing'.

So I add this, that one *cannot* give it. Oh, how my soul loathes the very odour of this stinking man-pleasing false doctrine that reeks everywhere around us. I cry, Then go on with your committal! I say, Go on with your 'acceptance' of Jesus. Blind guides! If you could do far more, such as giving your goods to feed the poor, and even giving your body to be burned, at the last you would but discover that it is not what you do towards God that makes God your salvation, it is not your activity at all: it is what God does towards you that makes God your salvation. It is your passivity altogether, it is the activity of Almighty God that makes the soul to melt, the heart to change, the mouth to open and the lips to cry, 'GOD is become my salvation'.

But even when the authority of scripture, the soundness of its words, is admitted, still salvation is not in saying these words, nor in being a self-styled champion of the doctrines of grace, neither in copying the words and books of dead saints; but it is actually to possess that which the words describe, so as the description fits our own real state. That is salvation. For the mere saying 'I am saved' is not at all the same thing as actually being saved. In fact, very often they are two entirely different things, the first being what man says, the second what God actually does. Only in the latter case can men justly say, 'God is become my salvation'.

Indeed, it is not the bare knowledge of the bible that is salvation. For that the bible and God are separate is evident. But it is GOD that is my salvation. If the bible alone saved, as well might the hardest sinner in the world buy a bible and keep it in his pocket and strictly charge his heirs to bury it with him: but that would not carry him to glory. His corpse *and* his bible will decay.

Neither will it do the soul any more good whatsoever for that same bible to be in the head rather than the pocket; no, not if one were buried with a headful of scripture. Though one fill mind and memory with every doctrine from the bible and learn diligently every major text in the bible, still the bible will not save one. For it does not say, 'The bible has become my salvation'. But it does say, 'God is become my salvation; therefore shall ye draw water out of the wells of salvation.'

Supposing you were absolutely clear on justification by faith. Even though you knew that article, even though you were never so sound and orthodox on election, even though you preached regeneration and held it as imperative that one must be born from above before entering the kingdom of God; even though you stood in a pulpit and preached the new birth and justification by faith—that would not save you. For it is not at all the profession, knowledge, preaching of the bible and its doctrines and exposition, however rightly interpreted and orthodox, to which the writer refers when he says, '*God* is my salvation'.

Truly God is ultimately—beyond the inspired writers used infallibly by him—the author of the bible, but one can have a thing an author has written, rightly interpreted, and yet be absolutely devoid of face to face, soul to soul, mind to mind, heart to heart, eye to eye, visible, real experimental acquaintance with the *person* who wrote it. God, he says, God *himself* is my salvation.

There are those who deceive multitudes: the bible, they think, is their salvation. But by such was Christ crucified. Saith Jesus to them: Ye Pharisees, ye search the scriptures; for in them ye *think* ye have eternal life. From the scriptures they thought to draw water from the wells of salvation but they were dry enough. For though they searched, and searched never so diligently, Jesus plainly says, 'Ye will not come to *me*, that ye might have life'.

I want to tell you this, I want to emphasize it, this is the truth: in that the prophet can say 'God is become my salvation'—*he* has not done anything. He did not do it. It is not by the letter of a few texts. Nor by diligent study of the whole bible. Not by acceptance. Nor by committal. Not by works or acts of any kind. Nor by letting Jesus in. This man did not do any such things. For in the will of the Father the Son out of his own deity called the sinner from the steeps of heaven by the divine Spirit, and by Godhead initiative became in Christ this man's salvation. Therefore with joy does he draw water out of the wells of salvation, because he knows it is *all of God and all of grace*. So I say that salvation is not by anything—anything at all—from man in any way whatsoever.

Now consider, That true Salvation is to know God the Father as one's Salvation

What then is the meaning of 'God is become my salvation'? What is it to have God as one's salvation? Isaiah saith not Messiah only; but God in and of himself. Not solely and exclusively the Lord Jesus, although no doubt the Son is included in this expression; but more: it is God in *three Persons*. Therefore, firstly, God the Father is one's salvation.

Although not known as such in the old testament, the revelation of the Father is what the prophet—mark that, the *prophet*—is foretelling and to which he looks forward: God the Father. For this, the Father's work in salvation, is something into which they that are saved can enter, can see eye to eye about, and over which they no longer have controversy. They can say that God the Father is their salvation by his eternal Purpose. Not by their purpose. It was not their purpose to turn to him. But it was God's purpose from eternity to turn them to himself. God, in the first instance, is their salvation as Father by his eternal purpose.

Secondly, God is their salvation by his immutable Will. It was not by their will choosing him. Because all must frankly confess, who own that they were saved of God, that they did *not* choose him but it was he that chose them! God knoweth.

I perceive that it is not of him that willeth, nor of him that runneth, but of God that showeth mercy. All who are saved are agreed, it is not of the will of the flesh, nor of the will of man, but of God. God is the one who dispenses his salvation by the working of his own immutable will according to his own eternal purpose. The Father is the one that reveals Christ; says the Son at Peter's confession: 'Flesh and blood hath not revealed it, *but my Father*.'

And again he saith, 'Every man that hath heard, and hath learned of the *Father*, cometh unto me.' Not by nature, nor by reason or works. Of himself no man can know the Son, turn to him, or come to him, so deep is man's natural depravity. But the Father knows the Son, and according to his immutable will reveals him to multitudes in salvation.

What a mercy! Hence if one knows God as one's salvation, one will be aware of the eternal purpose and also of the immutable will of God and the Father, and be deeply, profoundly, meltedly grateful for this revealed grace made known to oneself.

But not only so, for in the third instance salvation is by the determinate Counsel of God: oh, what a rich entrance does the saved soul gain into the counsels of God concerning his Son, and that seed chosen in him. What counsels were taken in Deity from eternity: what deep mysteries passed between one divine Person and another in the unity of the Godhead from everlasting, brought to light by the coming of the Son of God into the world.

Great is the mystery of godliness, and God, saith Paul the apostle, hath made known unto us the mystery: the Father has revealed his deep counsels—they all concern Christ, and they are all manifest in Fatherhood revealed, and they are all conveyed through salvation made known.

How secure it is to know God the Father as one's salvation: the fourth thing I would mention is that from eternity the

Father gave us to the Son, and determined to save us in an everlasting Covenant with him: this everlasting covenant between the Father and the Son, this is indeed salvation.

Moreover, fifth, the Oath of God and the Father confirmed this: By myself, saith God the Father, by myself have I sworn and will not repent. There is no feeling sense nor stable awareness of salvation till these things dawn on the soul and one can say, 'God is become my salvation'.

Moreover, as to the sixth point—of course I but touch upon these things in passing simply enumerating the wonderful soul-satisfying experiences made known by the Father—I say, God the Father becomes *our* salvation, when he makes known to our hearts his own Promise. He promises, he pledges, he lays his word to the line of eternal justice, openly promising beforehand to save every one of his trusting people. He will bring them at last to everlasting glory: justice is witness that he has publicly pledged himself. He has promulgated his word in advance, God has wholly committed himself before heaven and earth and hell, having made, spoken, recorded, written, and preserved his promise aforetime. By his promise he is pledged to save us.

The seventh way in which the Father is the salvation of his people is that he saves them according to the choice of his own eternal Election. 'According as he hath chosen us in him' —in Christ the Son—'before the foundation of the world.' It is an eternal election in love. Anybody that denies and fights this is fighting at the very fact of God being salvation. By his eternal election. By everlasting predestination. By gracious adoption. By giving us from eternity to the Son. By drawing us in time to the Son. For you know that it is not the law that brings you to Christ; the law prepares you to be brought to Christ, but it cannot bring you to Christ. What brings you to Christ is the Father. For no man can come to me, saith Christ in John, except the Father draw him.

Here is your modern evangelicalism: *You* open your heart! *You* make your committal! *You* let Jesus in! Ah, says Christ, 'No man can come to me, except the Father which hath sent me draw him.' And it is the sensation of these sweet drawings —'I have loved thee with an everlasting love: therefore with lovingkindness have I drawn thee'—I say, it is the experience of these things in the interior soul and the expression of them from the heart that ought to be opened and described in setting forth GOD's salvation: this, *this* is to cry, and cry indeed, 'Abba, Father'.

Therefore, if God has become one's salvation, what is seen first and foremost is the work of God and the Father in salvation. It is seen in the Father's purpose, in his will, in his counsel, in his covenant, in his oath, in his promise, and in his election: it is declared in the Father giving poor helpless sinners to the Son from eternity, in his making the Son their surety and substitution at Golgotha, and in his drawing them to Christ and in his revealing the Son to them, in point of time. This is indeed God's work.

Moreover observe, That true Salvation also is to know the Son of God as one's Salvation

But now to the next heading: not only is God my salvation in terms of God the Father, but since God is God in three Persons, it follows of necessity from the nature of God what—in actual practice — is experienced in process of salvation, namely, that God is my salvation in terms of God the Son. God and the Lord Jesus Christ are involved in the words, 'God is become my salvation'.

And there is a real, vital, and experimental sense of this. Oh, I know a soul may be never so simple, as yet never so ignorant of the terms, but from the nature of the experience of salvation, the soul cannot quarrel with the doctrine of it.

The truth will confirm his sensations not deny them, it will give cohesion to his conceptions not contradict them, it will but clothe his inclinations with sound words agreeable to his experience.

A new-born soul may not yet know anything about the oath, the promise, the covenant, the counsel of God in terms of doctrine; he may know nothing at first in terms of sound words about the will or the purpose, the foreknowledge and the calling of God: this—of a new-born soul—I confess freely.

The word election may be a mystery to him; predestination may be undiscerned, *but* he will sense and savour immediately upon the hearing and reading thereof that these are things in which he delights. He does not argue with election, he will hang upon it, for he feels within that if God had not chosen him he would surely have continued perpetually his rejection of God.

Although under emotional heat men may be persuaded to 'accept' Christ, yet as soon as relief begins to come or the soul matures, so soon will he turn back and give everything up in his heart. Oh, yes, after that he may become desperate again. In a moment of calamity then he will make new vows and promises to God. But as soon as the crisis is over, pressure is lifted and relief felt, why, then in comes the world again, back comes the flesh again, here comes the devil again, and all that never started is finished as usual.

And that is man. If it depends on man's choice, heaven will be empty and hell will be twice as full. So I say, for weak, helpless sinners, salvation has *got* to come from God for it cannot come from man. When salvation comes from God, the soul is aware it is all of God, as he is aware of God in and of himself.

It is wonderful, this instinctive consciousness of divine Persons on the part of even the newest-born soul. As soon as he is born of God, he is aware of three Persons in the Godhead: he can explain nothing yet he knows everything. He is a living example of the scriptures 'ye need not that any man teach you', and 'ye have an unction from the Holy One, and ye know all things'. Not for him the telling to 'know the Lord' for the Lord himself is his teacher. By experience he feels at first what afterwards he understands as doctrine. He is instinctively aware of his Father in heaven: he cries Abba, Father! and worships God.

He has been saved by the Lord Jesus and falls before him crying, 'My Lord and my God'. He knows there is one God, for God is his salvation experimentally. He knows there are three divine Persons in one, for the Father has saved him, and the Son has saved him, and the Holy Ghost has saved him, yet none but God has saved him. His stammering tongue cries in wonder, 'One thing I know, that, whereas I was blind, now I see.' This is the effect, the immediate effect, and the invariable effect when one believes on the Lord Jesus Christ and is saved: behold! God is become one's salvation.

The Son of God is firstly one's salvation because he received his own from the Father or ever the world was; he was the Surety of the Covenant before the world began, even from the mists of eternity. Believe it! It is true: he prays to the Father 'for them which thou hast given me; for they are thine'. He prays not for the world but for those whom 'thou gavest me out of the world'. Christ received from the Father from ancient eternity those whom the Father loved, chose, foresaw and foreknew, and whom he determined to save.

Christ received their names—'Thine they were, and thou gavest them me'—and before ever the Creation existed he pledged himself as their surety; yes, pledged himself for them all, unto the last single one of them. He is bound up with them in the bundle of life, he has long since given himself as their surety. He loved them with an everlasting love and he gave himself, standing in front of each one as the sword of legal justice was drawn against them: he interposed himself swiftly and bared his own breast. If it must smite them it shall do so through him. Since it must fall, then the cross shall show where it shall fall, and thus is demonstrated that he became their covenant surety.

But how could the Son do this if the Father had not first purposed it, resolved it, designed it? How, if God had not ordained it and God had not before determined him to be the sacrifice for his people? So we must commence with God the Father in salvation. For Christ could not be the substitutionary sin offering and judgment-bearer of his own poor people unless God had put him in that place. Or unless God was the one who made him to be sin, or unless God laid the sins of his people upon him, or unless God punished those sins, or yet unless God by Jesus' blood wrought out for his people a justification in righteousness. So I say, not only is the divine Son our salvation, but first and foremost God the Father is the Saviour of his people and he is so *by* Jesus Christ.

The Lord Jesus Christ in receiving the elect people of God from eternity unto himself, thus became the surety of the covenant by undertaking to save that people by himself as their covenant Head. Once having died for them, as risen and ascended he undertakes their salvation by declaring the gospel by the Spirit from on high, whence he speaks the doctrine as the Apostle of the new covenant.

Not as with the modern 'evangelical' view which supposes merely that since it is written in the bible, therefore reading whatever is written in the bible is to hear Christ speak. It is not. Now you say, Wait a minute. No! *You* wait. My meaning is this—when God inspired the writers to write, they wrote; and when that book is opened, the reader reads the inspired word of God: and very interesting one may find it to be to the mind. But when the Son of God, the actual present living Christ, speaks from heaven to the soul *by* that word, *then* the effect is heart-shattering, it is creative, it is regenerative, it is *alive*!

The holy scripture, the word of God, the inspired word of God is therefore a written record of the voice of God that the writers heard. Saith the prophet, The word of the LORD came unto me. And he wrote it. And without controversy it is from that once-written word that Christ speaks. But to read that writing is not the same thing as to hear his voice speaking by it. To read that writing is to read the unique record from which his spiritual voice now speaks: but between hearing and merely reading is a world of difference.

So when I say that the third office of the Lord Jesus Christ as our salvation is to declare gospel doctrine as the apostle of the new covenant, I mean that it is not the reading of what was then written infallibly by the apostolic pen on the page of the bible alone, though it is so written: it is actually to hear the voice of Christ by the gospel, personally, inwardly, spiritually, here and now.

Thus we read of Christ, 'He came and preached peace to you which were afar off.' But he is in heaven; how then can he preach peace on earth? I answer, when he moves his lips the faintest breath is caught by the Holy Ghost and carried down on the wings of everlasting love, and is breathed into the heart, and the same breath whispers in the heart and fans the inmost soul, so that one can say, The kisses of his mouth are most sweet. This experience is referred to in the exhortation, Today if ye will hear his voice, harden not your heart.

That is what I mean by Christ declaring gospel doctrine as the apostle—he does it himself: not only that he gave that doctrine by the apostles, nor only that since that time he sends his own preachers, but that throughout the age subsequently *he* speaks it to the heart. He does not say, My sheep read my word, though they do, but coming to the fountain-head, he says, 'My sheep hear my voice', which is another thing. That is my meaning. The Son of God must speak the words. Men will make a salvation of texts and think they trap God in printers' ink. But they, and their heaped-up teachers, are utterly at fault. The truth is, GOD is my salvation.

So you see that if one really knows God as Saviour, one will know that salvation in *God* the Son. And first, in his receiving us from the Father as the surety of his people, the surety of the covenant, for this *is* first with the divine Son in salvation. Next, in the counsels of the Godhead between Father, Son, and Holy Ghost, the Son from eternity undertook to save that people given him of the Father and to save them as their covenant head.

Then thirdly the Son of God saves us by declaring gospel doctrine as the apostle of the new testament; in the first instance in the giving of the holy scriptures, in the second by himself preparing—none of your petty little academies—and sending preachers, and finally, throughout the age as the ascended Christ by speaking those scriptures powerfully and internally into the heart.

Now the fourth office in which the Lord Jesus Christ becomes salvation to his saints is by his being the priest of the covenant. If men did but know it, out of the seething masses of this town—out of the indiscriminate ten thousands of the world in this place—at this very moment whilst you sit there hearing: Christ is on the throne of glory and he mentions in respect of this town not every name but certain names for whom he pleads. Chosen out of the world, they are those whom he once purchased and for whom now he intercedes. He shall triumph over them with salvation, being satisfied, absolutely satisfied, that he is abundantly able to call, keep, and preserve them, bringing them at last sanctified and holy unto his everlasting glory.

What a wonderful Saviour he is! But it is not the sentiment, it is the reality that matters. That which stands in the knowledge not of what I feel of him as Saviour, but of what he actually is as Saviour before God and the Father. However, you may see that it is not possible here to enlarge and explain each office of the Son of God: for this a book were required, and—if God permit—we hope in due course to provide the same.

But now time fails to tell of Christ in his saving offices: as of the One Mediator between God and man, or his being — sixthly—the true Sacrifice acceptable unto God, satisfying law and justice, fulfilling in one the Burnt Offering, the Meat Offering, the Peace Offering, the Sin Offering, the Wave Offering, and the Trespass Offering. The Yom Kippur, the Passover Lamb, the turtle-dove and the two sparrows: all is in Christ: Oh, Oh, what riches! In him are hid all the treasures of wisdom and knowledge.

Seventhly, he is ministered by the Holy Ghost in the knowledge of the gospel as the Substitute. He becomes in death, for the poor sinner, his substitution. This merit is administered, so that instead of the sinner at every time and in every point: Christ appears. In life and death, time and eternity, in mortality and immortality, on behalf of the poor sinner Christ hurries and rushes to interpose himself between God and that soul, and to stand in his place as a vicarious substitute.

Perpetually Christ doth interpose still and puts himself between the soul and God, always acting in a substitutionary office. In this, he is the same yesterday, today, and for ever. 'I am the LORD, I change not; therefore ye sons of Jacob are not consumed.'

He becomes our Justification by faith. Renouncing all supposed righteousness of our own by the law, and without any pretence to virtue, the ungodly are justified freely by grace. Discharged perpetually from the law, the very righteousness of God is imputed to their account. Everything is owed to the blood of Christ, my brethren: justification is wrought in blood alone.

He becomes our Propitiation by which God's wrath is appeased and he becomes altogether amiable and propitious towards us. He becomes our Ransom in which he sets us free from slavery and the place of bondage, having deliberately taken upon himself our chains, baring his back to the scourge and smiting of the awful taskmaster.

I say, he becomes our Remission by dismissing the sins of helpless sinners through receiving them into his body at the cross as though he had done them, but yet he did no evil neither was guile found in his mouth. He said, Give their sins to me. I say, before God, I cannot discharge my sins; but Christ said two thousand years ago, Give them to me. This is he who his own self bare our sins in his own body on the tree. Yes, and bare them all away. O! Sweet Saviour.

As God my Saviour, Christ becomes my Redemption in which I am loosed and set free. My Reconciliation in which I find myself in a new place altogether, under a new head and of a new realm. Christ becomes one's salvation by reigning in life now as one's Intercessor, one's Advocate, one's Teacher, one's Prophet, one's King, one's Shepherd, one's Beloved, one's Deliverer, one's Sanctification, one's Husband, one's Lord, and one's Kinsman.

Christ is displayed in all these offices by the Holy Ghost who leads the soul experimentally into the truth of them: the Spirit takes these things of Christ and shows them unto all his true people. By this you can tell that people: Christ is their All and they feelingly know and speak it, and time and eternity are short enough to find out his salvation.

Ah, say the worldly, You are too narrow. You are an old-fashioned extremist. You are unscientific. Full of old doctrine, you are a bigot and a fanatic. But actually it is the worldly that are narrow. Living on one dimension, heaven is shut to you, hell is hid from you, to the real nature of the world you are oblivious, and your sightless sockets gape vacant at time itself. Dead to God, blind to Christ, bereft of the Spirit, ignorant of immortality and insensitive to eternity: pray, *is* it I who am narrow?

Should they see the expansiveness which poor creatures who depend upon Christ behold—blest glories of his Person—they would say, Away with the trash of this passing gilded world! And so, too, would compromising modern 'evangelicals', that lean over backwards to accommodate the world, especially the young world, and only so that they may glory in the flesh for a passing season.

But what a future prospect opens up to them that are in Christ, whose salvation he has become. In shining hope Christ appears to the saints as the coming Saviour of the Body. The One who shall come again. Here are our politics! I tell you this, that Christ cometh again in the clouds with great glory. Under this heading he is, firstly, the coming Lord of Glory. He is the Heir of the world to come. Thirdly, he is the Resurrection. Fourthly, he is the Quickening Spirit. Fifthly, he is the Second Man. Sixthly, he is the Last Adam. Seventh, he is the Judge of All.

He is seen as the Bridegroom, as the Firstborn, as the King of kings, as the Lord of lords. He is viewed at first as the Alpha and at last as the Omega. He is discerned as the Root and Offspring of David. The Bright and Morning Star. He shines in hope as the Lamb on the throne, and the Son in the city.

So Christ appears to his own people, my dear friends, as Saviour, and is revealed to them in these offices. And as they grow experimentally and seek him as their All in all, he appears to them in *all* these offices. This is not their mere learning, it is their vital salvation.

Hath he appeared to you in any of these offices? And apart from this, has God the Father appeared to you as your salvation? If not, or if so far short, how can you say 'God is become my salvation'? And are you one of those that claim to teach others from out of your books? If so, it is revelation on humiliation that you need.

Finally it is to be emphasized, That true Salvation must include the knowledge of the Holy Ghost as one's Saviour.

I observe that salvation is not only of the Father and the Son, but also God as and in the Holy Ghost. God in three Persons, three Persons in one God. God becoming our salvation includes the Holy Ghost. Now—fully—therefore, all three divine Persons in one Godhead appear as our salvation. God the Holy Ghost is our salvation by his inward experimental work. Now, what an amazing range appears before our eyes.

How profound are the ways of the Spirit in bringing sinners to Christ. And again, how immense the magnitude of interior illumination—light and life—as he takes the things of Christ and shows them within the soul and to the heart. How magnificently he glorifies Christ, not speaking of himself, but always of Christ Jesus our Lord. All this he does both inwardly and experimentally by and under the sound of the word of the gospel.

How far removed this is from the cheap, the shoddy, and the utterly superficial modern gloss of self-absorption with so-called gifts. Our fathers in the faith did not so learn Christ. However, their children have mixed everything and hence they can discern nothing. But the truth is that not self but CHRIST is the one, in the DOCTRINE OF THE GOSPEL, about whom the Holy Ghost has come to speak, and it is into all the truth that he ever, only, always leads the saints. Never speaking of himself, never speaking of oneself: always HE GLORIFIES THE

Lord Jesus Christ by the gospel. By this you can tell the little flock.

When the Spirit brings sinners to the Lord Jesus, he does so because the Father chose them in Christ from before the foundation of the world by an eternal election, and he does so because Christ actually purchased them by the shedding of his own blood in an eternal redemption. Now at last in point of time the sinner dead in trespasses and sins, numb with unbelief, unfeeling, unenlightened, hard as the adamantine rock, now, I say, this ransomed sinner is to be brought to Christ in the full consciousness of vital union. What a divine task. What a mighty salvation this must be. However shall this be done? With man it is impossible but with God all things are possible.

First the Holy Ghost sends arrows of piercing alarm into the soul, 'Thine arrows stick fast in me', cries the alarmed sinner. Eternity looms, the Judgment appears, the blast of the trumpet reverberates throughout. Then it is that sin appears in the heinous iniquity of its true nature. The roll of thunder from Sinai ever and anon crashes into the ears of the soul, and Jehovah's lightning flashing from the holy law strikes the fear of God into the heart.

An Alarm! an Alarm! cries the soul. Now the Spirit echoes within from the preaching without of the terror of the Lord, of the flames of hell, of the torments of the damned, by the tiny band of the few faithful preachers still left to preach it. The alarming truth of the lost sinner's condition sounds as they cry aloud and spare not, but rather blow up the trumpet in the new moon of the soul with no uncertain sound, and moreover cease not to do so.

Thus these preachers preach with the Holy Ghost sent down from heaven. They take heed to themselves and unto the doctrine, for in so doing they both save themselves and those that hear them. The Holy Ghost works with them by signs following: heart-breaking permanent signs of the Spirit's interior working. Not the frothy effervescence of 'charismatic' waves of pretence, breaking ineffectually over the unchanged, gospel-rejecting, rocky heart of unbelief.

Now the soul is thoroughly awakened. Starting up from the sleep of death, eyes widen and hair stands on end, Job 4:15. God in judgment appears to thunder against the nature of sin, on his depraved and abused faculties, on the sins he has omitted and committed, on his false and rotten religion, on his love of flattering preaching, on his abuse of the truth. In consequence, the interior soul is wide awake to that which before was nothing more than a dream, in which he slept in worldly slumber and carnal ease.

How different now as he strains and strives at a gate too narrow for him and cries aloud for relief and mercy: but Oh, how alarming, how chilling: none appears, and the soul starts with fear, thoroughly awake, and sets to with a will to work up a righteousness of its own, and approve itself before God.

But now what convictions shake the soul. The Holy Ghost convinces him of sin, of righteousness, and of judgment to come, and, trembling at the word of the Lord, he cries, 'I am carnal, sold under sin'. He lays aside all his self-righteousness as filthy rags. He weeps, Not by works of righteousness which I have done, but after thy lovingkindness, O Lord, have mercy upon me. Broken-hearted he concludes, 'I can of mine own self do nothing.' 'My sore ran in the night, and ceased not.'

He lies like the paralytic at the pool of Bethesda, self-condemned and helpless, not daring to hope in God's mercy: in a word—as to all claims, self-reliance, all audacious and impudent expectations from God—he is slain. Self-condemned he has put himself beyond hope; he abhors himself in dust and ashes; his language is 'Depart from me; for I am a sinful man, O Lord'. Now, now and not until now, with this slaying work, God has the soul where he must be brought, and where God will bring in mercy if he is to be saved at all.

Yes, now when the soul is at its lowest, its deliverance is nearest. The Spirit surely will in pity soon cry to the soul:

> 'Thy warfare's past, thy mourning's o'er;
> Look up, for thou shalt weep no more.'

Now the quickening work takes place, and a soul-ravishing view of Christ crucified for sinners beams into the heart. Now it pleases God to call the convicted sinner by grace and reveal his Son to the inward heart, bringing joy unspeakable and full of glory. Now the burden rolls away because the blood of Jesus' cross is wonderfully nigh.

The soul forgets itself, JESUS CHRIST is seen and felt within to be one's very own Saviour and the Holy Ghost brings home the revelation in a mystery of love divine. Joy floods the soul, relief fills the heart, light illumines the mind, liberty the will, and an overwhelming sense of sweet distress, the agonizing ecstasy of pardoning love feelingly received, melts the inward parts, captivates the whole being, and whilst the mouth is filled with laughter the eyes overflow with inexpressible gratitude. Oh! Oh! it is a sweet pain but to speak the experience.

Then turns the soul, and the turning is that work of the Holy Ghost called Conversion. Faith follows, for Christ is so real, so seen, so felt, one so engrafted into him; the gospel now so precious, the doctrine so wonderful, preaching so desirable, obedience so natural, submission so delightful, that Repentance follows of course. The company of the real people of God are all one's pleasure. Delight and joy in praying make the soul to frequent oft both solitary place and likewise the prayer meeting.

Time fails to tell of the wonderful salvation brought home to the regenerate soul by the sanctifying Spirit of God. Suffice it to say here—though we trust to enlarge upon it elsewhere if God permit—that the Spirit renews, washes, fills, gifts, and graces the saints through his own indwelling presence. The effect of this is to glorify Christ, to elevate the doctrine, and to bring in God's eternal purpose by way of spiritual union.

As having been baptized by one Spirit into one body, the Holy Ghost ministers the saints' salvation together in the common faith. Dwelling as one in unity, brethren find themselves under the Anointing, subject to the Leading, drawn by the Earnest, grounded in the Establishment, knit through the Engrafting, transported by the Adoption, and vitalized through the Spirit of life. Under this unction from the Holy One they feel themselves in the strength of unity; they experience that they are sealed by the Spirit of God unto their eternal inheritance.

The world knows nothing of this. And, I may add, neither does the vast majority in the church. They should know better, but they have forgotten the old paths of their fathers. Neither can I see that all this 'coming out' has made any difference at all either. Not, that is, to the awful absence of this grand essential.

Certainly the great majority of the ministers know even less of this good, old-fashioned doctrine of salvation that used to be thundered, preached, and sweetly entreated the length and breadth of England. This was the tradition of the true and faithful gospel church right back to the apostles, plainly indicating their being built upon the one foundation of the faith.

On this rock Christ builds his church and the gates of hell shall not prevail against it. Let them raise both steeples, towers, and fabricated ecclesiastical edifices. Let them sit back, satisfied and full, withal in the palaces at Lambeth and Westminster and in their various Academies, Headquarters, and Centres.

But God alone knoweth the old paths and the ancient footsteps of the flock. The lowly Saviour brings salvation only according to the ways of God, other ways than those which stand in man's imagining, devising, and innovating. Salvation still stands in the grace of God, the power of the Spirit, and in the love of Christ. This not without but through a gospel which comes not in word only but in power also.

For it is God in three Persons that becomes our salvation. I say again to them that are young in the faith even if but newborn: He is so to you also: this doctrine will not stumble you—you shall delight in it. For you eschew by instinct what is shallow and false, and reach by a kind of divine affinity for the good old experimental preaching: Oh, may the Lord bless you greatly! May you find your thirst amply quenched by the waters of the Spirit. I know it will be so: for *God* has become your salvation.

Therefore, because God is our Saviour, because we trust in him, we are enabled to repose by faith on three divine Persons in the Godhead, trusting in a way of belief without works. Indeed we are dead to the law and have our backs steadfast against Sinai but our faces fixed to Zionward. I say, as resting by faith, the THEREFORE of verse three applies. Not in a demand for labour in order to haul up an empty vessel, but in a promise of grace as bringing in the Spirit. Because God—Father, Son, and Holy Ghost—has become our Saviour therefore of spontaneity water is drawn thereby.

So then, since God is become our salvation, it follows of course that, THEREFORE with joy shall we draw water out of the wells of salvation. So be it. Amen and Amen.

THE SECOND ADDRESS

The Second Address

And in that day thou shalt say, O LORD, I will praise thee: though thou wast angry with me, thine anger is turned away, and thou comfortedst me. Behold, God is my salvation; I will trust, and not be afraid: for the LORD JEHOVAH is my strength and my song; he also is become my salvation. Therefore with joy shall ye draw water out of the wells of salvation.

Isaiah 12:1-3.

1. The Location of the Wells

TO continue with the enquiry into the meaning of this place in the twelfth chapter of the prophecy of Isaiah and more particularly the exposition of the words, 'Therefore with joy shall ye draw water out of the wells of salvation'.

I have noted that drawing water out of the wells of salvation is peculiar to those who know God as the God of their salvation. In this connection I have shown what constitutes the knowledge of God as one's Saviour. Also I have observed that this experimental knowledge is precedent to drawing water from these wells. That is what the word 'therefore' indicates in this place.

It is not the mere textual knowledge of how salvation is described in and of itself—which would be solely an assent to the truth objectively—but it is the real subjective experience of salvation, it is actual knowledge from what God has done for one's own soul, and vouchsafed to one by God himself in an interior revelation.

Verses 1 and 2 — above — are introduced by a sovereign, saving, omniscient God foretelling what it is that 'In that day thou shalt say'. This is the Introduction. God declares by the prophet Isaiah the words which those who are saved will echo when God appears in time, to them, in their experience, as their Saviour. They will say, 'O LORD, I will praise thee: though thou wast angry with me, thine anger is turned away, and thou comfortedst me. Behold, God is my salvation; I will trust, and not be afraid: for the LORD JEHOVAH is my strength and my song; he also is become my salvation.' What God's people are foretold as saying in that day is therefore a prophetic quotation.

In verse 1 we see the awakening, the alarming, the convicting, and the mortifying work of the Spirit: 'Thou wast angry with me.' But soon is foretold the sweet relief of the gospel, the balm of Gilead for wounded sinners; for next follows a saving sight of Christ approaching the mourning soul: 'Thine anger is turned away.' Thus the sinner is drawn to the Lord Jesus for salvation.

It is not the law — verse 2 — but the Father who draws to Christ. The law prepares the soul for this drawing, by shattering all illusions about works and all notions of human virtue. But it is the Father who draws to Christ and causeth a sweet compliance and repose upon Christ Jesus through trust in the gospel. Christ is seen as the bleeding Lamb. The sinner hates his own works, mortifies the flesh, rejoices in the cross, and wholly trusts in Christ for salvation and strength. In seeing this and the joy it gives the soul, joy unspeakable and full of glory, he is led to say, 'He is my strength and my song; he also is become my salvation'.

Very well. But now observe that verse 3 reverts from the quoted *first person* speaking to God—to the *second person*, God speaking to us. The meaning is that because in a way of grace through faith we have been brought by the Spirit experimentally to say *that* to God, consequently—'therefore'—God says *this* of us: 'With joy shall ye draw water out of the wells of salvation.'

Hence notice that the change of person indicates, firstly, *that the verse is a Promise.* It is not something that we do as such, it is something which is assured to us and vouchsafed by God himself.

I repeat: a careful observation of verse 3 shows, from the change of person which I have indicated, that this verse is not a part of the foretold utterance of the saved. For the prophet returns from stating what 'in that day *thou* shalt say'—which statement is, of course, in the first person, 'I', 'my', 'me'—returns, I say, from that, to God's speech to us. It is not therefore what *we* address to him, but what *he* declares to us. Here is a declaration which is in consequence of our prior address to Godward. It is *then* that he promises, THEREFORE WITH JOY SHALL YE DRAW WATER OUT OF THE WELLS OF SALVATION.

Moreover the change of person indicates, secondly, *that the verse is an Imperative.* It is imperative from God to the praising, the healed, the comforted, the resting, the trusting, the reposing: 'Ye shall.' There is no if. It does not say 'Ye shall if ...' It is not, Ye may. Nor, Ye shall try. Not 'I hope ye shall', but, *Ye shall*!

Now I would point out that it does not say drink from the wells, but draw from them: you see that such liberality is indicated that more than one can possibly drink is drawn up on any given occasion. Withal, what vast reservoirs remain below, no matter how often or how much one draws. As if that were not enough—no mere cup of cold water given by men to a disciple this—God indicates the abundant extravagance of his bounty by the fact that it is not simply one well from which water is drawn: the plurality indicates a plenitude of wells.

Further to this, notice that it is from Wells that water is to be drawn: not from the streams for example, but wells specifically. Neither from the brooks. Nor from the rivers. Not from the still waters but from the wells of salvation. Brooks meander, you see. Rivers flow across vast territories. With these there is such latitude of location: they stretch for miles. Besides, rivers are visible, the water is plain for all the world to see. Again, lush vegetation and arable pastures are about their whole winding length.

None of these things is true of wells. Wells are different. Wells are fixed: dogmatically at a fixed point we can say, *there* it is and it is *all* there. There is no room for latitude or compromise about which stretch we mean! More, the water is invisible, not displayed for all the world to see. Again, it is when this world is a desert that wells are found. These things establish the wells. By these features they are distinguished.

It does not say, Ye shall *dig* wells, mark. They have been dug: it is not that persons and meetings dig their own! For others have laboured, and we are entered into their labour. You must *discover* these wells, find the water, and then draw that water. Recorded in the word of God, Abraham, Isaac, and Jacob were the diggers of wells and Abraham was the original digger of wells. Now all these things happened for our ensample, having a spiritual significance, as we shall see.

'Our father Jacob gave us the well', said the woman of Samaria, but does that really matter to us? Yes, because what that well signifies is the spiritual well from which Jesus gives the water of life. The well therefore is a type or figure of the location out of which in fact we receive the water of everlasting life. The well is not the water, mark, it is the *place* where there is a *way* to the water.

Notice, in passing, what spiritual events were synonymous with the digging of the wells. Look unto Abraham. He is the hewn rock and the hole of the pit whence we were dug, says Isaiah. What shall we say that Abraham, our father, hath found? enquires Paul. A well, is the answer. Those wells which Abraham dug were for generations to come. Look unto Abraham and Sarah that bare you.

Wells are holes which are sunk in dry and arid terrain. They are for a dry and thirsty land where no water is. Naturally there is neither knowledge nor hope of reaching underground water which is totally hidden and which is not seen from the surface. There is not a clue that anything is there. In the ancient world, cities were built around rivers, watering places, and known wells, and there the world settled. But Abraham was told of God, 'Get thee out of thy country, and from thy kindred, and from thy father's house, unto a land that I will show thee.'

And he was shown a land but no water was in it, there was a famine in which nothing could live. He walked alone in the howling wilderness and discovered wells in the most unlikely places, removed from those sources out of which the world drew its water and its sustenance. Abraham had been separated from the cities of this world and whence should he find water in this wilderness?—from the God of providence leading him to the right location and the doctrine of Christ instructing him where to dig, withal the supply of the Spirit confirming that word with the outpoured water of life.

So then, with regard to wells in the desert there are three things which it is essential to observe. The first of course is the *location* of the well. You cannot draw water until you first find the well. This must hold good spiritually and to this I intend to return later dealing with what Abraham and his children found in the way of wells.

Next there is the *content* of the well. In our text this is not in respect of literal water but in respect of what is intended spiritually by the idea of water. That is, as literal water answers to the bodily craving—a craving which if not slaked and satisfied will become completely overwhelming to the point where one can be sent raving mad from thirst—so there is this spiritual analogy. The first question is, Where is this water? Answers the prophet: In the wells of salvation. The next question is, What is this water? The reply is, it answers spiritually to the craving of the soul, as that water which is physical applies to the thirst of the body. As natural water is necessary to the body so is this spiritual water essential to the soul.

Many people have never been in a desert. Many people have never been without water. Many people have never experienced what real thirst is and certainly that holds good in counterpart spiritually. They have never been brought to a point when they would willingly throw away their money, their goods, their houses, their lands—everything they have in order to get this one thing. As the woman at the well at Samaria said to Jesus, Sir, Give me this water. Anything for this!

Hence physical thirst finds its deeper counterpart in that breathless unquenched drought created in the soul by the Holy Ghost, and so saith the psalmist, 'As the hart panteth after the water brooks, so panteth my soul after thee, O God'. The world knows absolutely nothing of these ardent inward yearnings, and, tragically, they are not found in the backslidden professing people of God either.

A backsliding people can endure to live without God. The contented world lives without God, but in contrast there is a genuinely spiritual people who have this interior thirst, a thirst that only water from the wells of salvation can assuage and which nothing but being filled with the Spirit can satisfy.

So there is a similarity between physical and spiritual thirst. As between water and the Holy Ghost. Thus we see that not only must we locate the wells, and that by infallible direction, but also there must be the creation of soul thirst—otherwise this water will be despised. And then finally there must be a bringing up of the content of the wells.

The third thing then is the *drawing* of this water. As the woman of Samaria said to Jesus, when he sat by the well, 'Sir, thou hast nothing to draw with, and the well is deep'. She thought, how are *you* going to get water out? But he said to her what she never expected by way of a reply, for she expected him to humble himself according to the necessity of what she supposed to be his great thirst, and say to her in pleading tones, Well, would you please draw for me? Because, you see, she had the rope and the vessel.

But what he said in fact was this: 'If thou knewest the gift of God, and who it is that saith to thee, Give me to drink; thou wouldest have asked of him, and he would have given thee living water.' For 'whosoever drinketh of this water'—in the well of Jacob—'shall thirst again: but whosoever drinketh of the water that I shall give him shall never thirst; but the water that I shall give him shall be in him a well of water springing up into everlasting life.'

From these three simple observations it will be seen that everything depends upon the discovery of the wells. The location of the wells is the primary consideration; the first and great point of enquiry must be, Where are these wells located, and what is their spiritual significance? To this end notice that the wells of salvation were already extant even before the prophet wrote these words in Isaiah 12:3. Isaiah referred to what had been known for some thousands of years when he wrote, 'Therefore with joy shall ye draw water out of the wells of salvation'. Isaiah did not say, Ye shall *dig* wells of salvation, but implied to those to whom he first spake, Ye shall draw water from wells as it were already long opened and dug.

And since it is true that not unto themselves but unto us the prophets did minister these things, therefore it pertains to us as well as them to locate these wells, albeit owning how difficult this may prove to be because they are neither material nor tangible. To locate what is invisible and spiritual admittedly is difficult. But it is not so difficult that it cannot be done, and thirsty souls have found and surely will find the way to do it, for that is the gospel method. Indeed it is what the gospel is for: to locate these things in terms of clear truth and doctrine that once were symbolized by type and picture in the figures of the true in the old testament.

Now I say that these allegorical, these evangelical, these invisible wells which in spiritual things fulfil exactly the same function as an actual well in material things, these can be located. Albeit Isaiah referred back to literal wells in the old testament—speaking of the wells of salvation—he did so in order to suggest to the minds of the spiritual the invisible reality which those figures were intended to convey. Not to refer to the mere figures in and of themselves. Isaiah did not mean his readers to understand the material type of the actual wells, but the spiritual antitype of what those wells represent in terms of the truth. Hence they are 'of salvation'.

And this is true of the water. The point is what that water represents. Everything must be distinguished and the meaning discerned. The well is not the water, it is where the water is found. It is not merely the vital hole in the ground but it is water drawn up therefrom which satisfies the thirsty soul. Now the truth depicted by this figure of water—signifying the giving of the Holy Ghost—is that it is found here in the wells of apostolic doctrine and nowhere else.

You need not think, for example, that you can go to any indiscriminate religious meeting, or to any sect, group, denomination of your mere choice, or to any church irrespective, or arbitrarily hear any preacher you fancy; thinking, 'Oh well, this is a church, and that is a preacher, so no doubt I shall find the wells of salvation and doubtless there is going to be water discovered to my soul.' Oh no. In fact, you are far more likely to be deluded than satisfied.

You see, as I have said already, long before the new testament commenced or the church began these wells had already been declared, so they are an infallible touchstone prior to and greater than the name Church or the function Preacher. The bare name and mere function mean nothing: the reality of salvation either justifies or condemns them both, and not the other way round.

Therefore my problem and yours is one of discrimination, or spiritual discernment from holy writ, in order that we should not gullibly swallow anything and everything. We must not be mistaken over this, for it is the most vital matter in heaven and earth, time and eternity, for our immortal souls: finding the wells of salvation and drawing of water therefrom. Now precisely because this is so vital these wells have been long, long since both plainly marked out and clearly described.

We need be under no doubt about it, we need be under no misapprehension, this is not a matter of arbitrary choice, not open to the conclusion of individual human opinion. It is rather a question of authoritative divine direction. If Isaiah the prophet indicated long before the coming of Christ that there should be a drawing of water from already dug, clearly located, plainly defined wells, then we need have no doubt what they are, where they are, or precisely what is meant by them.

It is not our prerogative or that of any church to devise and open our own wells. We *have* done so, as Israel did before, and broken cisterns have all these proved to be at that. For it is to our bitter shame that following the papists, both Protestant and nonconformist churches in measure—though not so great measure—have turned to broken cisterns, not even the Brethren being exempt. We have *all* erred and like lost sheep gone astray and failed, and so often after more and more increasingly auspicious beginnings, and we must cry: 'I have sinned and thy people ...'

But I say, the humble and heart-broken penitent need not be in any doubt or under any misapprehension at all, for it does not pertain to ecclesiastical opinion or to man's notion or a preacher's imagination or to the church's option or to denominational preference to say, This is the well we prefer and choose, drink ye at it. For the wells of salvation have already been opened once for all and set forth long, long ago, before the church began. Do you understand? He that hath ears to hear, let him hear.

2. The Excavation of the Wells

Now the question is, If the wells of salvation—which we are not to dig, but to draw from—were in type already opened and excavated before Isaiah the prophet wrote, when, and by whom were they dug? And lest we should seem to be preaching our own opinion let us show that it was all of God that they were dug by those whom he afore chose to this work, namely those elect who acted not in their own will but as directed by God himself, in consequence of which the revealed title of what they excavated was declared to be The Wells of Salvation.

Furthermore it must be seen that those types, fulfilled, are in fact the wells from which Isaiah himself drew water and that the patriarchs, fathers, and the old testament saints drew water out of them too. Wells which the Lord Jesus himself showed forth, from which Peter and Paul, John and the apostles drew water. From which the early church and the new testament saints drew water.

If we can once prove this, then I say we have declared unto you the sole and only wells of salvation and the point is established. It is to these wells and these alone that the true church and faithful preachers are to testify. By this gospel testimony and the drawing of water therefrom the true wells may be distinguished from the false cisterns and from mere traditional sandy depressions.

Actually these words of Isaiah applied to Israel from his very beginnings. The *truth* of these words applied in fact in Genesis, although the *utterance* of them was reserved till Isaiah the prophet declared them to Zion. In chapter 12 verse 6 we read, 'Cry out and shout, thou inhabitant of Zion: for great is the Holy One *of Israel* in the midst of thee.' These words were spoken of God to *Israel* as such, that people whom Jehovah took up by election in the old testament, and having taken them up, in the process of time then prophesied to them saying, 'Ye shall draw water out of the wells of salvation'.

What is this but that since these wells were known to the prophet and to the contemporary children of Israel, then at least in type they already existed? And if so, then they must have been dug by the *fathers* of those children, for whilst there are numerous references to the patriarchs digging wells, there are virtually none of any of the children so doing.

Hence in John chapter four the woman says to Jesus, who does not contradict her, 'Our father Jacob gave us the well'! Jacob, whose name you will remember was changed to Israel—'Thy name shall be called no more Jacob, but Israel'—and who begat the children of Israel to which hundreds of years later Isaiah prophesied and cried, 'Great is the Holy One of *Israel* in the midst of *thee*'! And, 'With joy shall *ye* draw water out of the wells of salvation.'

Now father Jacob, or Israel, gave us this well, says the woman at the well of Samaria, and since Jacob's father was Isaac, and

Isaac's Abraham, we can say quite clearly that these were they who dug the wells in the beginning, who were also the first to draw water where previously there was none.

For until this hole was let down into the dry, barren ground, no one knew that water was there. But by some spiritual discernment, by some divine impulse—not by some natural gift, not by a forked stick or a trembling bit of iron—directly by the revelation of God, Abraham felt at certain crises in his life that he must dig this well or that, and this signified and answered to spiritual experiences he had undergone.

So that since Abraham went through certain spiritual exercises which then God satisfied, and at such times also found himself in the desert in need of water, then by revelation was shown a well, it is not surprising that he associated the finding of wells with the parallel of his spiritual experience, and so did the prophet. For just as that well saved his body, so the experience brought salvation to his soul. So as that well was the well of salvation to his body, this well was the well of salvation to his soul.

These spiritual things which were first revealed to Abraham had never been revealed before, they were unknown, so likewise those wells were arid desert before Abraham dug them, no one had any idea hidden things existed, nothing was there but dry, baked, dusty sameness. It is out of what such wells signify spiritually in the gospel that ye shall draw water, and out of no other, for there are no other; and if you will not draw from these wells you may be absolutely certain you shall surely perish world without end, finding nothing but scorching, empty, and bleak wastes throughout eternity.

Furthermore, the prophet directs the people to the wells of salvation which were located and dug by Abraham, Isaac, and Jacob when he states in Isaiah 51:1,2, 'Look unto the rock whence ye are hewn, and to the hole of the pit whence ye are digged. Look unto Abraham your father, and unto Sarah that bare you: for I called him alone, and blessed him, and increased him.' Clearly showing that the hole of the pit—the original well-digger to whom they were to look for the wells of salvation—was Abraham their father.

My final conclusion to establish the truth that the wells of salvation are those dug spiritually by Abraham, Isaac, and Jacob, stems from the fact that the word 'well' in the old testament finds its inception and its origin in the book of Genesis with the digging of Abraham. His name in fact is the first name in the bible with which the word 'well' is associated.

Surely this suggests that the 'wells of salvation' are those signified by the wells which were physically dug out at or about the time that these saving truths were revealed to Abraham, Isaac, and Jacob. So much so that God is called, The God of Abraham, Isaac, and Jacob. What ancient roots anchor our gospel!

We have no need of a 'novelty' gospel. We have no need of gimmicks in the church, we have no need of any fancy innovation. We deal with deep soul truths. We deal with the revelation of God and if men have changed after a fashion, he has not. If fashion has altered, his fashion has not altered. The relationships between the soul of man and the God of his salvation are the same.

Therefore, since those things were originally shown in the beginning, our safety lies in being one hundred per cent apostolically traditional, spiritually orthodox, and biblically conservative. We have our proofs settled and stable from the fact that these things have been tried not merely for centuries but for millennia; so that to depart from them now in the end of the world would be the most crass ignorance and folly that can possibly be imagined.

3. The Delineation of the Wells

The Wells of salvation, then, signify not those openings in a sandy desert, but rather the penetrations into divine truth which the patriarchs disclosed. By these through faith should flow and indeed veritably gush the waters of the Holy Ghost, in a spiritual refreshing unto eternal life. This is that of which the Lord Jesus spake when he cried: 'If any man thirst, let him come unto me, and drink. He that believeth on me, as the scripture hath said, out of his belly shall flow rivers of living water.' This spake he of the Spirit. Of these things the wells were typical, and strictly only fulfilled in the Lord Jesus himself; but the doctrine and witness of them was plainly declared in Abraham, the Father of the Faithful.

Now I say, the first of the chosen seed in the land of promise was Abraham—in whom the gospel was fully depicted—and he was followed by Isaac and Jacob. I would point out that this was long before Moses came, and that therefore not a particle of the gospel could possibly owe one jot or tittle to Moses. Abraham was justified by faith with a righteousness which was imputed and which obtained over four centuries before the law was instituted or promulgated by Moses.

For the scripture testifies plainly that the law was *not* in the world at this time. The *idea* of a righteousness that is obtained solely on the basis of the scholastic theory of so-called 'active and passive obedience to the law' is no ancient well; it is a novel puddle faintly depressing upon the recent sands of time. Such an academic notion is unscriptural, illegal, and unevangelical. Abraham knew nothing of it, nor did the righteousness of God with which he was freely justified by grace through faith in 'the Lamb slain from the foundation of the world'. A world, remark, oblivious of the law till long, long after Abraham.

What shall we say, then, that Abraham our father hath found? Why, that a man was justified by faith *without* the law or its works, and that this justifying righteousness came by promise alone before the law was given or typified. Hence such a righteousness, already fully revealed, could not possibly be wrought out on a legal principle. Although of course justifying righteousness fully meets and satisfies every curse of the law that came in by and by. But it transcends the righteousness of the law as high as heaven is above the earth.

So I say that long before Moses came or the law was given, Abraham was even then justified by faith and was fully persuaded that this free righteousness should come to him by faith through promise only. So 'God preached before the gospel unto Abraham' as the third chapter of Galatians assures us, seeing that 'to Abraham and his seed were the promises made'. 'And this I say, that the'—new—'covenant, that was confirmed before of God in Christ'—to Abraham—'the law, which was four hundred and thirty years after, cannot disannul, that it should make the promise of none effect.' What a well of salvation is here.

But how can one receive a righteousness when one is unrighteous? Abraham knew that he could not justify himself before God. By what righteousness then should he be justified freely and that by grace? By the righteousness of God. To demonstrate the manner of this, God caused him to take, slaughter, and divide the chosen sacrifice and to do so even with his own hands.

Thus he stood all blood-stained amidst the pieces of the slain creatures, standing between the rent and divided carcases, betwixt the two sides of an heifer of three years old and those of a she-goat of three years old and a ram of three years old and two young birds—he stood, I say—amidst the slaughtered sacrifice, in the midst of the butchered pieces, standing on the blood-stained ground. There God as it were testified to him, Thus shall the righteousness of God be wrought out by sacrifice alone, and so shalt thou be justified by blood only. Nothing added before, and nothing after.

Then, in the midst of that sacrifice already made, and as on the ground of that shedding of blood showing forth the satisfaction of divine righteousness in a vicarious offering, a horror of great darkness passed over chosen Abraham: which darkness and horror signified the coming in of the law four hundred and thirty years later.

For the legal rule was also seen to be fully satisfied at the place of atonement, in the very place where God reconciled eternal justice and divine mercy, where he brought in everlasting righteousness. There I say, there the curse of the law was also met, and in death redemption from the law itself was obtained. This was to Abraham a revelation like an opened well not sunk down in earth but paradoxically opened up into heaven. Thence the waters of the Spirit flowed down: there the windows of heaven were opened: so was the blessing of God shed onto one below who had not room enough to contain the outpouring.

You see that these wells of saving disclosure into gospel truth were revealed long before the legal system came. Not only are they openings into the high doctrine of God but they are as it were gospel penetrations through earthly barriers into the soul, the inside of which with regard to the experimental knowledge of God is as dry and hard and lifeless as the Qattara Depression.

The soul is as arid as the Kalahari, it is as waterless and dead and as blasted as the depths of the Gobi, it is absolutely barren of any penetration towards God. You see, it is not you who dig the wells, it is God who from the other side opens everything up to you. That is salvation. 'God', says the prophet, 'is my salvation'.

It is not a question of free-will digging to God; it is a question of God—having first met and answered all the objective obstacles to salvation, then—excavating and sinking the wells down to the helpless until on the inside of the soul the earth quivers with the force of his digging. It cracks, finally breaches, light appears, the earth rattles down, and finally God has got through to one.

That is salvation! 'God is become my salvation.' It is through these wells, through this opening in the packed, hard, dry, barren earth of the soul—The first man *is* of the earth, earthy—it is through these wells between the soul and God in Christ Jesus that the Spirit flows and the angels ascend and descend upon the Son of man over an open heaven.

Yes, it is these gospel penetrations into heaven towards God, and then let down through earthly barriers into men, through these that there flows the water of life, and hence Isaiah calls them 'The Wells of Salvation'. Certainly it is a joyful thing to draw water through them. There is no question about that. That is experience, not what you read about, debate over, or argue around; it happens to you, and you know it.

These wells were revealed to Abraham, Isaac, and Jacob in a saving way. As I said to you, the gospel of salvation to their souls was as water in the desert to their bodies. So clearly and so much was the gospel before preached and revealed unto Abraham—those thousands of long years before the coming of Christ and indeed also hundreds of years before the giving of the law at Sinai—that in the omniscience of God the most intricate, specific, and tiny details of the gospel were illuminated. Then how much more its massive principles were most plainly manifest, in order that we in these last times by Abraham might have the clearest possible evangelical instruction.

I say, so much was the gospel before revealed unto the patriarchs that God is called by the Lord Jesus himself, several times, the God of Abraham, the God of Isaac, and the God of Jacob: so much was he their God. They were the actual makers of scriptural history, they dug the typical wells themselves, they were unique.

So God refers to himself as theirs because by them first the truth came to light. Saith Jesus, He is not the God of the dead, but of the living, for he *is* the God of Abraham, Isaac, and Jacob. He is not ashamed to be called their God. God is not the god of this world, as the world fondly imagines, but the God of pilgrims and strangers who look for a world to come, an heavenly country, an holy city. There is no question of their trying to better the world with an invented 'social gospel'. It is not a matter of bettering this evil condemned world, it is rather a matter of renouncing the world and fleeing from the wrath to come.

Indeed the world supposes that God is not only the god of the worldly, but so confused do they suppose him to be that they think he is the god of Buddha, the god of all outward Christendom, the god of Mohammed, the god of the Heathen, the god of the Apostate also, and the god of all Arians, Socinians, Pelagians, Unitarians, and of anything else at all provided that it is contrary to sound doctrine.

But we are utterly separate from such foolish and ignorant notions, and so was Abraham, for God was known as Abraham's God, not the god of this world. God was concerned with saving Abraham from the world not losing Abraham in the world. With making Abraham dead to the world not dead with the world. So that with Paul Abraham might say, 'But God forbid that I should glory, save in the cross of our Lord Jesus Christ, by whom the world is crucified unto me, and I unto the world.'

Indeed, Abraham and his seed are as strangers and pilgrims on the earth, not fellow-citizens and residents. Abraham was not a politician, he was a pilgrim. He was a patriarch not a patchwork manufacturer. He was not a man with a god so general he was no god at all, he was a man with God so personal that God actually and specifically named himself *Abraham's* God, and Abraham's Friend.

The acts of God to Abraham were what made God his God. God did things to him and with him and for him, and these actual specific acts from heaven to earth for Abraham alone, created a unique relationship because they were singular acts done to no one else: it is *that* which makes it *correct* to say, God is one's God.

God took this man and God became his God. He was Abraham's God: God took *Abraham*. Now the LORD had said unto Abram, 'Get thee out of thy country, and from thy kindred.' He would not reveal himself in the old worldly context. He was not the god of Abraham's kindred. 'And from thy father's house.' He was not the god of his father's house. 'Unto a land that I will show thee. And I will make of thee a great nation, and I will bless thee.' And Abraham's friend! And Father! The God of Abraham, not the god of the world.

God was not ashamed to be the God of Abraham and his seed for ever, and they were not ashamed to own God with a relationship so intimate, so personal, and so vital that it could be said, 'This God is *our* God for ever and ever: he will be our guide even unto death'. 'O God of *my* salvation, God.' That is the way God is known, my friends. This is a well of salvation. This is life eternal, said Jesus, that they might know thee, the only true God, and Jesus Christ whom thou hast sent.

God was not even the God of all Abraham's seed. God is never called the God of Ishmael, though Ishmael was born of Abraham's loins and God heard the plea of his parents. But God never called himself Ishmael's God. He is not the God of Ishmael. He is the God of Isaac, as it is written, 'In Isaac shall thy seed be called.' *God* chooses whose God he will be, not man. That is the thing. Have you got a hold of that truth? Oh, says someone, I don't like that truth. Well, I say to you, you will not find the wells of salvation without it. What man does is to reject God perpetually and incorrigibly. What God does is to choose according to his own electing purpose in grace.

God chooses his people. He is not the God of Ishmael, much less the God of Esau, for he testifies, 'Jacob have I loved, but Esau have I hated'. And Esau, with tears streaming down his face, sobs and cries and yearns to have God for his God, but God turned his back upon him. Mind you, there were good reasons in Esau for that, because it was what Esau had *lost* that filled him with remorse too late, for Esau despised a future inheritance and only wanted what God *gave* now, not God *himself* nor the world to come. But it is still the truth that God hated Esau. There were just as good reasons in Jacob whereby he might have been hated, but God chose Jacob: Jacob have I loved.

This love of God is particular and electing, free and distinguishing. Indeed God so loved the world in a general way that he gave his Son to display his goodness before the face of all men, even of such as Esau and of Ishmael, but this only brings to light men's hateful character. Man of himself both spurns the God of love and despises the love of God, in favour of himself and the world that now is. That is mankind, and it is when this enmity comes to light by the universal rejection of God's love and kindness, that then, then appears both the eternal election and the perpetual reprobation of God set forth in Jacob and Esau.

So you see that as to purpose God displayed his love in general that he might extend his sovereign electing love in particular. Thus he procures Jacob, his Israel, his chosen people, and withal brings to light the enmity of man by nature that he might manifest his wrath as well as display his grace to the elect. And these he will procure and draw with an everlasting love and with the cords of lovingkindness, and this nothing shall prevent.

God is the God of a chosen seed. Not the God of the dead, said Jesus, but the God of the living. Why? Well, these have been quickened in Christ Jesus by the Spirit and have got the living waters, you see. They have got to the wells of salvation, they have not quarrelled with them. They have no arguments with free grace. They have laid down the weapons of their rebellion. They have found their depravity, put off the enmity of the old carnal mind. They have got to the wells of salvation and to the living waters. He is not called the God of Adam, my dear friends, I can assure you, but the God and Father of our Lord Jesus Christ, and in Christ the God and Father of those given unto Christ before the foundation of the world. This God is our God for ever.

It is one thing to have the form of religion, and one thing to have the form of the church, but it is quite another thing to have present the God of salvation and the living God within that church. Then the living waters flow through and from the assembly; hence the question is, Whose God is he? The answer is, he is the God of that living people whom he creates and quickens, not the God of that dead people who draw near to him with their lips but whose unchanged, worldly, hardened, barren, and arid hearts are far from him. In consequence of their own will and choice, such hypocrites are wells without water, plucked up by the roots, twice dead, and without fruit.

You may say, that is critical. But is it penetrating? It may move up a lot of rubbish, but what do you expect if the wells of God are going to be cleared and re-named according to the names given by father Abraham? For God *is* the God of Abraham, 'the father of us all', that is, all that are raised out of the death and lifelessness of nature to life in the Holy Ghost. He is the God of all those that are ordained unto eternal life. I *give* unto them eternal life, says Jesus, and, Out of their belly shall flow rivers of living water. In them is a well of water springing up unto eternal life. He is the God of the living, even to as many as Jesus gives eternal life, to as many as are ordained unto eternal life. He has become their God, and says the scripture, he is also the God of their salvation.

Now that is a remarkable statement, because you would think that God would be the God of a person only, not something done *for* that person as well. But in fact God not only calls himself their God, but also 'the God of their salvation'. His deity presides over saving them. He looks at poor, helpless, weak, corrupt, lost sinners with a naturally incorrigible root of iniquity within, O, such a stinking fountain of rotten corruption which they cannot hide but have to confess, and then he calls them '*my* people' and he says, 'I am their God'. But *them*!

Moreover he says, 'And I am the God of their salvation.' That is, he pledges his deity in respect of their salvation, his almighty divinity presides over saving their fallible humanity. Oh! Who will win the unequal strife? Will we cast ourselves away from him? Yes, if we can. Will we fall away in apostate sin for ever? Yes, left to our own selves. That is what man does, his will being corrupt he cannot keep his grasp on salvation. Away with rotten Arminianism. Yet withal, come nigh trembling, careful, fall-fearing, watchful perseverance.

But God is the God of our salvation. That is stronger than our rotten will, our incorrigible iniquity: ALMIGHTY GOD pledges omnipotent deity to preside over *all our salvation and to effect it, despite ourselves, from first to last.*

No wonder the psalmist—lost in wonder, love, and praise—cries aloud, and the sweet psalmist of Israel gives forth: 'O God of my salvation, God'!

Almighty God rules omnipotently over the salvation of his people, as says Isaiah 12:2, '*He* also is become my salvation.' So it is no wonder that the prophet continues, 'Therefore with joy shall ye draw water out of the wells of salvation'.

Yes indeed, my beloved brethren, it is all fulfilled. And now why tarriest thou? Arise, and drink. For the promise is nigh unto you and to your children; yea, unto them that are afar off, even to as many as the Lord our God shall call: 'And the Spirit and the bride say, Come. And let him that heareth say, Come. And let him that is athirst come. And whosoever will, let him take the water of life freely.'

The grace of our Lord Jesus Christ be with you all. Amen.

THE THIRD ADDRESS

The Third Address

1. Now let us consider the Hebrew word 'beer': translated 'well' in the Authorized Bible

IN the old testament we find the single English word 'Well' used to translate several distinct Hebrew words for this subject. In fact the Hebrew original gives as many as five *different* words for the basic idea of 'Well'. This distinction is of course lost to the ordinary reader, because of the one indiscriminate English rendering for the varied Hebrew meanings.

So it behoves the minister of the word to open up these hidden and different aspects, to show why they have been employed respectively, and to give some distinctive examples of their use. Then the delicate nuance and fine shade of meaning peculiar to each Hebrew word will no longer remain undetected by nor hidden from the English reader.

The effect of this will be to bring one into a discerning sense of how material and visible things were made by the Holy Ghost to serve spiritual ends. It will give one an insight into the experiences of the old saints who were so fully in accord with the mind of the Spirit. Finally it will immerse one in the heavenly atmosphere that surrounded the discovery by the patriarchs of the wells of salvation and the water of life.

The first thing to which I would draw your attention is really a family of words: *beer*, *bor*, and *baar* — to transliterate the

Hebrew—and in fact this word *beer* is the one mainly used in Genesis to signify the wells dug by Abraham, Isaac, and Jacob. It is to these ancient wells—transcended into the typical and spiritual—that the prophet Isaiah refers, when he speaks of 'The Wells of Salvation'.

The word *beer*, although used for a well of water, does not refer to the well-water as such; the reference is to the pit rather than to the contents. Strictly the *shaft* of the well is indicated. To illustrate this I observe that the related word *bor* is also used for a 'dungeon'. A pit or dungeon. Hence in this context, the idea is that of a well of water coming to light by digging a pit.

Indeed, one may go further and say that it is not so much the pit as the digging of it that the word *beer* really has in mind. A dug pit. In fact the Hebrew root of this family of words conveys the idea of: 'to dig; cut upon; cut into.' Hence, of course, since the shaft of a well is dug, cut upon, cut into, then *beer* is used to denote a well. Not because of the water at all, but because a well is 'dug' or 'cut into' in the Hebrew.

Such words lend themselves to figurative use. The metaphor immediately appeals to the perceptive reader. For example, *bor* is used in Jeremiah 2:13: 'They have forsaken me the fountain of living waters, and hewed them out *cisterns*, broken *cisterns*.' Although they no more literally hewed cisterns than others literally drew water from the wells of salvation. But that figure so suited what they were doing in a way of what was spiritual—or unspiritual!—that nothing was more apt than to say, 'They have forsaken me the fountain of living waters, and hewed them out cisterns, broken cisterns'.

Observe how Jeremiah adapts this word *bor* which denotes 'pit' and is derived from 'cut into'. For it was not as if there were any water in what backsliding Israel had 'dug out'. All the water was to be found in the fountain of living waters. But this they forsook and hewed for themselves *bor*; but, by definition, these are mere empty shafts. Water is not implied at all, for of themselves, *bor* are bone-dry pits. So, you see, the Hebrew word is admirably suited to figurative use.

Another instance of figurative use, by means of the association of ideas transferred from the physical facts concerning material things to their spiritual counterpart in the things of God, appears especially in the case of the word '*baar*'. Not exactly *beer*, notice, but *baar*. However the common stock of both words immediately appears to the eye. Especially when one considers that there are no proper vowels in written Hebrew.

The word *baar* means 'to declare' or 'make plain': in other words, 'dig down' so as to expose hidden depths. In this case the use of the basic idea 'to dig, cut into', bears by association the nuance of 'to dig into *the meaning*', 'to make clear *the truth*', 'to expose to light *the hidden spiritual depths*'. Yet it is the same basic conception as that indicating the wells which Abraham dug.

As an example of this word, notice Deuteronomy 1:5, '... began Moses to declare—*baar*—this law.' He cut into it. He opened it up. He exposed the word of the Lord from the scripture. He cut it open in the sight of all the people so that they could see what it really meant. He got the word of God and he cut it open. He dug it out, and there was water there! In a figure, he made it a well. Do you understand? He made it a well.

Those who go and do likewise, to this day, follow in the steps of the prophet who spoke first of spiritual wells, of Abraham the first well-digger, and of Moses the exponent who brought the meaning to light. They are able to take the word of God and open it up, so as the springing well of the Spirit refreshes the pilgrim people of God with living water.

Moreover in Deuteronomy 27:8 we read: 'And thou shalt write upon the stones all the words of this law *very plainly*.'

That is the word *baar*. Dig it right out, do you understand? Expose it completely. Likewise Habakkuk chapter 2 and verse 2 reads: 'Write the vision, and make it *plain—baar—*upon tables, that he may run that readeth it ... the just shall live by faith', v.4. Now if justification by faith is not a Well of Salvation, what is? But Romans 4 makes plain that it was *Abraham* through whom first the well of justifying righteousness came to light.

In confirmation of this, I observe that Isaiah advises us, 'Hearken to me, ye that follow after righteousness', Isaiah 51:1. There it is, the righteousness of faith, justification by faith. The prophet then points to the original uncovering of that righteousness: 'Ye that seek the LORD: look unto the rock whence ye are hewn, and to the hole of the *pit—bor—*whence ye are digged.' He explains his meaning by continuing immediately: 'Look unto *Abraham* your father.'

But why the term 'Wells of Salvation'? Because the gospel revelation to the panting heart and dry soul of father Abraham came with the same sweet relief—the identical thirst-quenching ease—as did the gushing waters from the *bor* to the temporal salvation of his burning tongue and parched flesh. Since both experiences were made known uniquely to the patriarch, what could be more natural than to associate ideas and identify the gospel truths revealed to Abraham under the figure of 'Wells of Salvation'?

Have you not today seen these wells, where they are, and what they are? Is it not absolutely clear to you beyond a peradventure? Is it not cut into, dug out, exposed, and made plain? Surely, therefore, these are the *beer*, the wells, the plainly revealed places out of which Abraham got water. Certainly it is so. Yes, rightly expounded, cut into: *beer*.

And indeed, speaking of exponents, one might mention Hosea the prophet. His name implies '*Salvation*', and since the name of his father—Beeri—means 'My *Well*', there is no doubt that we can expect great things from the pen of this suffering prophet. Hosea was wonderfully enabled to open up the love of God, and clearly he drew water from the wells of salvation. He is a pre-eminent example of the fact that the true exponent lets down his own shafts—'*my* well'—through the exterior dead letter into the rich truth that underlies it, out of which then begins to flow the water of life in a springing well unto salvation.

(i) Abraham's well: BEERSHEBA, and its spiritual significance

But now let me return, particularly, to recount that which Abraham our father hath found. What truths came to light as and when he dug wells for water in the wilderness? Very many in every way. As an example consider the digging of Beersheba. You must remember that Abraham dug Beersheba? Abraham said to the Philistine, 'Witness unto me, that *I* have digged this well', Genesis 21:30.

Previously Abimelech the Philistine had discovered that God's election was no mere theory, and he hasted through bitter experience to exchange gifts of peace—despite his unchanged enmity—with chosen Abraham by the well Beersheba. For a start, election has a witness at the well. And water flows. And the envy and enmity of the world is witnessed to also, and separation withal, for Abraham had set apart seven ewe lambs and it was a witness to Abimelech the Philistine that his servants had stolen Abraham's well: stolen it!

Abraham had left Beersheba for a time, and when he came back, the Philistines had stolen the well. Yet Abraham was the one who had told his servants at the beginning where to dig for water. Afterwards, however, the Philistines came and camped round about, so that on Abraham's return they were found to be occupying his well. The Philistines hadn't dug it, they had stolen it: Abraham dug it. Notwithstanding, seeing that the Philistines were determined upon contention, Abraham rather suffered himself to be defrauded, and departed the place, pursuing the way of peace.

Now of course the Philistines closely watched Abraham to see whether he would fight or not. What was he going to do about it? He did nothing. It was God that vindicated chosen Abraham. And so the Philistines learned that God *was* the God of Abraham. Even when the patriarch was altogether at fault, as in the matter of Sarah his wife—although God chastened Abraham sore—yet still over and above it all God blessed him. Thus the Philistines wot that whom God blesses *is* blessed.

And they began to find all kinds of things going wrong with them. So they found something else to wot as well, namely, that whom God curses *is* cursed. Then they concluded that if they made Abraham their enemy, they made God their enemy, and it went ill with them for Abraham's sake.

Hence—experience having taught them not to meddle with Abraham—they sought a covenant of peace with him. Meanwhile quite forgetting all about the stolen well, naturally! Very convenient. Abimelech had three thoughts: Enough of this strife; Let us make a covenant of peace; What stolen well? Let us have covenant, you see—try and forget the well—but let us make covenant. Benignly, Abraham responded, proposing the well Beersheba as the place for the covenant of peace. There! No doubt Abimelech thought, Preferably elsewhere.

But evidently Abraham prevailed for they took oath just by the well; one feels that nobody was looking at it, doubtless very carefully looking in the other direction. Thus they made covenant for future peace and exchanged gifts at Beersheba. Finally Abimelech, seeing all the presents had passed from one to the other, cried out, 'What mean these seven ewe lambs which thou hast set by themselves?'.

Well, these seven ewe lambs right in front of Abimelech appeared to be nothing to do with the oath: but why were they there then? The Philistine tried not to say anything, being a man of the world. You know the attitude: I'm not curious in the least, I couldn't care less, I'm not interested. Seven ewe lambs! *Pah*! But in the end he could not contain himself: 'What do these mean?'. What *on earth* are these standing outside the tent all this time? What mean these seven ewe lambs set alone?

Oh, responds Abraham, that's just to show that this well is mine. That rather beclouded the scene. However, Abimelech bowed to the justice of Abraham's gentle reminder, and received the gift in acknowledgement of Abraham's truth and his own deceit. Thereafter the well was named from that incident—*beer*: the well; *sheba*: of the oath—Beer-sheba. For they took an oath that day that this *was* Abraham's well, and the seven ewe lambs were a witness to Abimelech that it was Abraham's well.

It is significant that we do not read of Abraham or of his servants digging wells until after his major spiritual experiences. For example, after the birth of Isaac. Although as a matter of fact in the account of Isaac's sojourning we read of many wells which his father had dug that are not mentioned in the actual account of Abraham's pilgrimage. Abraham during his lifetime dug those wells, but they are not recorded in the narrative of his life. Deliberately they are left out.

In fact they come to light in the life of his son. This is as though to suggest that the important wells discovered by Abraham were not those literal wells which quenched his natural thirst, but rather the saving wells of truth which Abraham left as an evangelical inheritance to his posterity. These 'Wells of Salvation' came to be associated with a few of those literal wells dug or visited around and about the time of Abraham's experience of that salvation.

So by these we are directed to those spiritual insights into otherwise hidden and unrevealed truths for which Abraham's *soul* thirsted. These openings, once they were manifested, brought into Abraham's interior life a springing well of thirst-quenching divine experience which flowed from God to his inner being. By this living water a union was entered into and felt, and a sweet savour of the coming Christ Jesus made known. I say these spiritual openings to otherwise barren depths of the soul brought a life-giving stream by which God made himself known to the hidden man of the heart. These are the wells that are the important wells in Abraham's life, and these the real heritage that Abraham left to his son Isaac and to his seed for ever.

Consider Isaac's life also. Just as God blessed Abraham, so likewise blessed he the chosen seed Isaac, and moreover cursed his enemies also. This latter was something which struck the Philistines and struck them deeply; yet the way he prospered, on the other hand, filled them with envy. They did not like to see Isaac prosper.

So in Genesis 26:15 we find that the Philistines stopped and filled with earth the wells which Abraham his father had dug. Some seven ewes! Some oath! So is the word of this world, and so you will find it in experience. Thus also will you find true in the end what Paul knew best at the beginning: God forbid, he says, that I should glory, save in the cross of our Lord Jesus Christ, by whom the world is crucified unto me and I unto the world.

However, the world still retains many gilded and flattering views of itself. To this day—as if the cross meant nothing—it professes so many moral presumptions, proclaims such elevated notions of itself. The world slumbers on with noble idealism. But such an infatuation practically proclaims that the world quite dispenses with reality in self-conceited dreams of virtue.

In truth the 'educated' world is bloated with high-flown theories of human virtue; it is hoary with vain religious hypocrisy; it is saturated with social philosophies and political dialectics, flattering to men. All of which quite blinds the eye of the deceived to the actual realities. The cross shows what the world is really worth. In the judgment of God the moral worth of the world is set forth vicariously in the despised Saviour hanging rejected upon the cross for the sin of the world. This love is what the world despises; and then pretends to virtue? How gladly the enlightened can say: 'By whom the world is crucified unto me, and I unto the world.'

It has always been so: the Philistines of this world ever exhibit the same malice towards Abraham and his seed. So it was with Isaac. When Isaac departed from the wells of Abraham his father, the Philistines in their hatred came and stopped the wells which Isaac had just left, filling them with their filthy rubbish. No doubt they would have attacked Isaac openly, but they wot that 'whom thou cursest is cursed'. So their snide and cowardly methods were oblique: not from any respect or love of law; their restraint—such as it was—was motivated by fear and fear only: they had no love of virtue whatever in their dark souls.

However, in chapter 26 verse 18 we read: Isaac digged them again! which was very irritating and a grievous thing to the Philistines, for they had just taken all that trouble to fill them in: and I can tell you it is very irritating to a Philistine when his filthy rubbish is all taken out again. They don't like it, and they don't like the chosen digger either. No, they do not care for pure gospel wells: they prefer moral muck, philosophical filth, or putrid religious rubbish: that is what *they* put in place of the gospel.

For you see, Philistines are full of theories for society; they have great plans to educate, as they call it, the people. But then they have this problem. The problem is the gospel. It must be taken away, and its place filled with their theories. Then there is the problem of the preachers of the gospel: these reminders of old Abraham whom they had thought of as dead in every way. Philistines detest these foolish preachers who have the impertinence still to believe this old-fashioned gospel stuff. Such people they regard as the arch-enemies of the liberty of evolving men and women: or men and men: or women and women.

Why, they cry indignantly, for all our mass-educational method and application, there are those still remaining who have the impudence to believe God directly created the world! Heresy! they froth. As to Noah and the flood: at the very sound they faint clean away for anger. And regarding any reminder of what they consider clean covered-up and well-filled with evolutionary dirt, any reminder, that is, of the antique biblical notion of Adam and the Fall: Well! It is all too, too much for the liberals of spiritual Sodom and Gomorrah. As to the Fall, total depravity, election, salvation, and all this blood as well—if these things should be mentioned to them all at once: why, veritably they are in danger from apoplexy.

So the Philistines stopped the wells, filled them with rubbish, and then renamed them with false names. But Isaac carefully followed them around and digged them again, and, says the scripture, renamed them after the names which Abraham his father had given them. He gives the wells their right names as well as digging out the Philistine muck. Oh, were they in a temper! They really fluttered their left wing, and their right one too; naturally, academically, politically, religiously, and sociologically.

And over the past few generations to this very day the Philistines in the church have—metaphorically—filled the wells of salvation with disgusting substitutes for the pure gospel: with no better than moral compost and spiritual manure. That is why you will hardly hear the word 'SALVATION' ringing out in the church today. Why not? Because they do not believe there is anything to be *saved from* that priests, psychiatrists, pseudo-ministers, sociologists, evangelistic entertainers, and charismatic comedians can't handle.

The Philistines that have filled the church—as anciently they captured the land of Israel—have not only filled up the wonderful wells of salvation, but also the dread and awful reality of hell they have covered over, the flames of everlasting judgment against sinners they think to have beaten out, and the vengeance of eternal fire they suppose to have smothered. Thus the *reason* for the sacrifice of Christ they have earthed over again with their foul diversions. See, then, how well the description suits today's 'evangelicals': 'dumb dogs, they cannot bark.'

Instead of the solemn praying for and preaching of salvation, the Philistines and their many fellow-travellers have filled up the vacuum with their humanizing sentiment, pathetic platitudes, and their feeble compromise. All well larded, of course, with 'messages in song', 'family services', petite chic sermonettes, teenage trifles, and suchlike things as they do, the meanwhile dispensing those cheap bribes whereby they ingratiate themselves with indifferent men, silly women, and simple children. What bribes are these? Such as the unspoken promise, assured to those who support them, that such will certainly not be disturbed by the truth of the gospel. Nor will there be any possibility of hearing of the dread danger of being lost. Or of the agonizing need of eternal salvation from the wrath to come.

Of necessity therefore they have reduced what they call 'preaching' to about a quarter of an hour of weak moralizing. And even that fifteen minutes they conduct with jocularity. Oh, they have filled in the wells of salvation with their levity and their lightness and their loose behaviour, winking and walking delicately as Agag with their worldly compromise. They are replete through worldly associations, supine in worldly ease, and gorged with worldly pleasures. They are absolutely full: they have filled in the wells of Abraham full of rubbish. Rubbish! But see! Yet the Lord will raise up a Samuel to cut down with the sword of the LORD these uncircumcised who put darkness for light and who clean pervert the gospel of Christ.

Therefore, in principle, modern Philistines fill up the measure of their fathers to this very day. Just as they did in Isaac's time with regard to the wells of his father, so the moral offspring of the Philistines continue to do over the wells of salvation to the spiritual remnant that is left. They have done it to us over what our fathers had uncovered. Read the old preachers, enquire of the old ways, look to the old landmarks, and see what has been lost.

And not content with that, even the good old English bible itself the academic Philistines have dared to smear with rubbish and call a 'translation'. Yes? 'Translated' from their own invented text. What a damp squib! This novelty text of scissor-wielding liberal theoreticians is no more than an amalgam of discarded remnants either rejected by the proper authorities, hoarded by greedy papists, or languishing in monkish waste-paper baskets. Behold a miserable firework filled with scholastic greed, wrapped with droppings from a monastic dustbin, mounted on the fatuous bandwagon of the evolutionists, and fired from the sputtering candle of gasping academic ambition. And do they call this novelty scholarship? If you want scholarship, read Burgon.

Yet for all the havoc these people have wrought, and the ghastly train they have set in motion, be assured that even to this latest day you will find those who walk in the old paths. Such recognize new errors, and are those who, having tasted the old manna, soon detect the modern poison. Whereas others who are carried about with every wind of doctrine, infatuated with every novel trifle, charmed with each whimsical fashion:

why, naturally, it is in character for them to shout the praises of modern deviations from both the Textus Receptus and from the Authorized Version.

Some bastard—not true-born—Calvinists are of this sort. See their bedfellows! For you will find the perverted translation also used by neo-papists, Palagians, Socinians, and Arminians. Used too by self-styled 'evangelists'—the modern mendicant begging-friars. You will find it used in charlatan meetings, cheapjack meetings, degrading-Christ meetings, and dishonouring-the-gospel meetings. In fine, the Philistine Version will be used wherever novelty is the rule. But all this shabby garbage shall utterly diminish when once is lifted up the dignity of a pure and true religion and withal a tried, sure, and *HOLY* bible.

For there *is* a remnant of the Salt of the Earth that is left, discernible in that they utterly repudiate what the Philistines of this present generation have done. And moreover they repudiate it in the name of Almighty God. This remnant stands by the Good Old Book. Therefore it is a remnant which still owns and testifies that the church is entirely spiritual in her concept, authorized in her bible, uncompromising in her doctrine, exclusive in her discipline, divine in her worship, and separate in her walk. In short, a remnant wholly concerned with the salvation of God for the world to come.

(ii) Isaac's first well: ESEK, and its spiritual significance

Isaac and his spiritual heirs to this day infuriate the Philistines by digging out the muck from the wells of Abraham. And this seed is not merely negative but equally positive for we read also, Genesis 26:19, 'Isaac's servants digged in the valley'. That is, quite apart from Abraham, you see, *Isaac's* servants digged in the valley.

When Isaac had finished opening up all Abraham's wells—as comprehending Abraham's experience, as knowing the right names for the wells, and as having drawn water therefrom—then Isaac went on and dug his own wells also. Isaac's servants digged in the valley and found another well. So Isaac, in a place of deep depression and gloom, the valley of the shadow, finds a well of salvation for himself. In those very circumstances. But when the Philistines saw what he did they strove for his well; and Isaac called the name of that well Esek, which means 'strife' or 'contention'.

And so it is today. Although these modern Philistines get nothing from the dry earth of their dead ministry, from the dead text of the bare face of the bible, yet when we by our own labour go down into the valley and dig a well and are given our own springing fountain out of it, then they contend with us in envious sourness. Which is the truth.

(iii) Isaac's second well: SITNAH, and its spiritual significance

Notice that in Genesis 26:21 Isaac's servants yield the well of contention, Esek, and then they go and dig another well in another place. But the Philistines promptly leave the one which Isaac peaceably yielded to them and forthwith they follow Isaac to his new well. They leave the well about which they had been so desperate before. Oh, they are not interested in water: they are only interested in preventing him getting what they aren't given. That is all they are interested in: as it was from the beginning, is now, and ever shall be till God separate the sheep from the goats.

You can see that the Philistines are doing everything possible to seek occasion against Isaac. This is nothing other than the fulfilment for that time of Galatians 4:29: 'But as then he that was born after the flesh persecuted him that was born after the Spirit, even so it is now.' The Philistines, unable to dig their own wells, cannot stand that Isaac should dig and prosper by the blessing of God.

To the Philistines it is unbearable that the heirs of promise should have all this water. It fills them with anger. They drive them from well to well. But on goes Isaac in peace, and once again he finds and his servants dig wells the previous existence of which was totally unsuspected. This is most irritating to the carnal Philistines and for this they hate Isaac, in that God blessed him but did not bless them. Seeing this enmity Isaac calls the next well Sitnah, which means 'hatred'. And you who are spiritual, marvel not if the world hate you.

If you draw water out of the wells of salvation, and if your pilgrimage is by way of the wells of Abraham and Isaac I can tell you this: you will be no friend of the world, and the world will be no friend of yours. As I told you before, so now I tell you again: they that are after the flesh—in religion, mark—shall persecute them that are after the Spirit, and that till the end of time. Saith the scripture, The friendship of the world is enmity with God.

Prophesies the Lord Jesus, The time cometh when they will cast you out of the synagogues. Yea, the time cometh when he that killeth you will think he does God service—says Jesus—will think he does *God* service! He will think he does. But on the other hand, Rejoice and be exceeding glad, for so persecuted they the prophets—and Isaac too—which were before you. Yes, even the very persecution—'Esek', 'Sitnah'—marks the wells of salvation. You may safely count on it, they that are not persecuted, are not the chosen seed either. For these are things that always accompany salvation.

(iv) Isaac's third well: REHOBOTH, *and its spiritual significance*

In Genesis 26:22 Isaac removes to a place where the Philistines were absolutely certain that he was finished. Well, there is no possibility of water there! Even he cannot dig a well there! He leaves the valleys where one expects the water and he is driven to a miserable, barren corner of the land, where, as they would say, there is not a hope of water; no question of any water at all.

So Isaac departs, and then there is no more strife. Simply because the Philistines are assured of his downfall. They watch from the edge of this barren wilderness, waiting for Isaac's humiliating fall in that sour, unwanted corner of the land, to which they themselves had driven him. But Isaac digged another well even there. *And* he gets water out. And when they see this they are afraid to proceed further, for they perceive that this thing is of God. It is too much. This whole thing is of *God*.

Yes, Isaac digged another well even there. And do you know the name of that well? The name of that well is Rehoboth: 'For now the LORD hath made room for us, and we shall be fruitful in the land.' The name Rehoboth means 'enlargement'. But in and of itself it is such a barren, dry place that this cannot come to pass with what is naturally true of this harsh land. Notwithstanding, supernaturally the wilderness and the solitary place shall rejoice for them, and the desert shall rejoice and blossom as the rose; behold, and see it come to pass that the mirage shall become a pool.

It is a case of 'Sing, O barren, thou that didst not bear', for what is spiritual shall, as separate and distinct, flourish and prosper. Now Isaac has arrived where there is no possibility of worldly help, no room for the flesh to glory and none for natural growth to develop. This is where God would have his chosen people. Rehoboth! They shall flourish from the singular and miraculous blessing of God alone: Rehoboth! Thus Isaac, who had been driven from pillar to post by the Philistines for standing by the old paths of the faith, by the old wells of Abraham, and in the old ways of the Lord, was vindicated at Rehoboth.

And in many ways we cannot but see a parallel in the way in which this little flock at Bethlehem Meeting Hall has been driven from pillar to post for holding to the old ways in the midst of a faithless church that has forgotten the God of our salvation and the gospel of our salvation. Driven from pillar to post we found to our astonishment when God gave us this derelict chapel an old stone over the door on which was discernible the word 'REHOBOTH'—enlargement. 'For now the LORD hath made room for us, and we shall be fruitful in the land.'

So I do advise you to pitch your moving tent a day's march nearer home, my dear friends; for as the man said, I wot whom thou blessest is blessed and whom thou cursest is cursed. And God swears to the seed in Christ to this very day—for spiritual Abraham has not gone yet—Surely blessing I will bless thee and multiplying I will multiply thee.

And it is the truth. It is absolutely true. I can assure you of the truth of it but I can tell you this, that it takes a lot longer than you think. You would like it to happen sooner; but when you are young then you learn from God that this is the time of discipline, to sit quiet and learn in subjection, but the vision will come, and will not tarry. Wait for it, for it is for an appointed time and it is still true. 'Blessing I will bless thee.'

I say, despite all the Philistines in all the churches and all the lawlessness out of them, still God enables a people joyfully to draw water out of the wells of salvation in the place of all places where you would think that surely they'll get nothing there. But they have got their wells even there and particularly there. Rehoboth!

(v) Isaac's fourth well at BEERSHEBA and its spiritual significance

Finally, Isaac goes to Beersheba of Abraham, and God appears to him there. God appears to *him* there. He digs his own well in that very place. Isaac did not have to call that the well of Abraham, my friends, for it was not. It was his, tapping the same hidden reservoir, guided by the prior experience of his father, true, but achieved through *his own digging*.

How many today are merely historical reviewers of Reformers, Puritans, Nonconformists, Brethren. They have nothing, but nothing, for themselves. However, Isaac actually compassed his father's experience and got water out for himself by his own digging. This is Abraham's true seed. Not of man, neither by men, but directly and experimentally by Jesus Christ and God the Father.

So this word '*beer*' is the first of five Hebrew words for 'well'. Now I think you may see plainly from these few random instances that the literal wells are figurative of the spiritual openings God gave unto the patriarchs. As a whole and in principle, physical succour through actual wells was used to prefigure and typify that spiritual salvation of God in Christ conveyed by the Holy Ghost through the gospel under the new testament.

Thus the wells of salvation convey, for example, the revelation of justification by faith; what it is to prove oneself in experience chosen of God; what it is to know the Father's oath of blessing; what it is to see God vindicate the peacemaker: such are the things encompassed by the figure. In fine, wells of salvation are here, and they are perpetually experienced by the elect seed in every generation.

2. Consider the Hebrew word 'mayan': translated 'well' in the Authorized Bible

But now I must pass on to the next Hebrew word similarly translated 'well' in English. This word, *mayan*, is one of the most significant and it is actually the word used in Isaiah 12:3.

The prophet uses the word *mayan* because it refers not to the pit—*beer* or *bor*—but to the *water* which that pit contains.

A very closely related form of this word aptly illustrates this distinction: 'And David longed, and said, Oh that one would give me drink of the water—*mayim*—of the well—*bor*—of Bethlehem, which is by the gate!', II Samuel 23:15. Through his bodily thirst David indicated that for which his soul craved: it was for *that* water that David longed, from *that* well. By means of the physical facts David indicates his spiritual longing: and this speaks of his desire for Christ.

'But thou, *Bethlehem Ephratah*'—Ephratah hints of the Opening of Bethlehem, where David locates the well—'though thou be little among the thousands of Judah, yet out of thee shall he come forth unto me that is to be ruler in Israel; whose goings forth have been from of old, from everlasting', Micah 5:2. He who should come of Bethlehem in Judah would give water which if a man drank thereof, he should never thirst again. David intuitively felt this and his natural thirst was the occasion of spiritual expression. 'He that believeth on me, *as the scripture hath said*, out of his belly shall flow rivers of living water.'

This is the kind of water figured in the Hebrew *mayan*, which means literally 'a fountain'. It is not the shaft of a well that is defined by this word, but rather the effect which that shaft has when it reaches water that is under pressure, or water that is pent up. The water bubbles up, it is a fountain, it is living water. The *beer* or *bor* releases the pressure, the digging down breaks through, and the water spurts out. The untold relief which this brings to the weary and thirsty desert traveller is indicated in the words: 'Therefore with joy shall ye draw water out of the wells of salvation.'

The distinction is clear: *beer* refers to the digging, and has to do with excavation and bringing to light, but *mayan* refers to living water thus reached and released. It bursts out, it is a fountain. This well-water called in the Hebrew *mayan*, a fountain, is gained at no small cost, as signified in David, II Samuel 23:16,17. 'And the three mighty men brake through the host of the Philistines, and drew water out of the well of Bethlehem, that was by the gate, and took it, and brought it to David: nevertheless he would not drink thereof, but poured it out unto the LORD. And he said, Be it far from me, O LORD, that I should do this: is not this the blood of the men that went in jeopardy of their lives? Therefore he would not drink it. These things did these three mighty men.'

And of this cost writes the psalmist in the eighty-fourth psalm, declaring in the sixth verse, 'Who passing through the valley of Baca—weeping—make it *a well*.' So then they who go to Zion must of necessity pass through the valley of tears; yet, however, the sorrow passes as a dream and the mouth soon fills with laughter. Though going forth weeping doubtless such shall come again with joy, for, 'With joy shall—they—draw water out of the wells—*mayan*—of salvation.'

The wells of salvation undoubtedly refer to the doctrine of Christ, for it is by faith in him that the waters of the Holy Ghost flow abundantly. Thus we read of God's work in Christ under the figure of the Rock of our Salvation, Psalm 114:8, 'Which turned the rock into a standing water, the flint into a fountain—*mayan*—of waters'.

God does this; it is *God* who turns the Rock into a standing water and the flint into a fountain of waters. Moses' rod—the legal rule of rectitude—never, never could bring forth water. Only the broken law must be satisfied in justice, and Moses must needs strike the Rock to show that this was so. But when *God* himself on his own account smote the rock, then it split indeed. And, says the scripture, *God* turneth the rock into a standing water and the flint into a fountain of waters. He did this when Moses—as signifying the law—struck the rock on behalf of the broken law. *Then* it was that God smote the same in divine righteousness according to the infinite measure of his own eternal wrath.

All this we see fulfilled at the cross and its consequence at Pentecost. For, confirms the apostle Paul, I Corinthians 10:4, 'That Rock was Christ'. He declares: 'They did all drink the same spiritual drink: for they drank of that spiritual Rock that followed them: and that Rock was Christ.' But by then it was smitten: and that smiting was the cross, as the flowing was Pentecost. Do you understand these things, who profess the Christian religion? If not, consider, why not? 'Uneducated' fishermen, 'illiterate' slaves, the poor of the earth, our own rustic fathers, honest Huntington, and bluff old Bunyan: to them it was an open book.

Then again we read—Psalm 87:7—that the spiritual man's fountain is Christ. 'All my springs—*mayan*—are in thee.' All of them. Not some of them in mother and father, husband or wife. Not half of them in nature, not some in this present world. Not the heavenly springs in thee but the earthly in house, home, family, in business, in ministry, in church; no, no, 'ALL my springs are in *thee*'.

Hence it is written, Luke 14:26,27: 'If any man come to me, and hate not his father, and mother, and wife, and children, and brethren, and sisters, yea, and his own life also, he cannot be my disciple. And whosoever doth not bear his cross, and come after me, cannot be my disciple', so saith Jesus. Therefore all Christ's own have *all* their springs in him. Somebody says to me, You ought to qualify that. Oh? It is obvious where such persons' springs are: forever qualifying the gospel, taking words out of Christ's mouth, putting others into it: with what are such persons left, but their own deceitful fabrication?

But all the spiritual man's springs are in Christ. Because from the commencement of the work of God in his soul such an one is shut up in the valley of weeping so that bitter experience and sheer soul travail shall teach him that it must be from Christ and Christ alone that all his supply is to be drawn.

Neither can minister, church, or even the letter of scripture be anything but broken cisterns in the matter, no, nor can parents be of any value in this spiritual exercise: the same with husband and the same with wife. Every empty vessel of man you that are spiritual shall lick dry as bone till your very tongue rasps down to the parched floor of the pit of every human resource. Then shall you prove in experience that everything outside of Christ is a waterless mirage. It is inwardly from Christ that you must get relief, out of him alone that you must drink the waters of salvation.

But to proceed. The word *mayan*, in fact, has been translated Fountain sixteen times; twice Spring; and five times Well. The word actually comes from the Hebrew root *ayin* which itself also has been translated 'well'. One can see a similarity between the two words, and in this case appearances are not deceptive. Apart from the addition of the 'm', there is simply the apparent change in one vowel sound: *(m)ayan* from the root *ayin*.

Now *ayin* has been translated 'well' in the English bible some ten times. On the other hand it has also been translated 'eye' four hundred and ninety-seven times. Again, although this root *ayin* is used for 'fountain' eleven times, it is also used for 'sight'—what is perceived by the eye—two hundred and seventeen times. So you see that you are getting at the root of these things, you are getting at the pictures behind the words in the Hebrew tongue.

Thus this word *ayin* may refer to an eye, obviously. It may refer to the sight, clearly. It may refer to the judgment—what one can see rightly—because judgment is a question of sight and whether one's eyes are open to all that is to be seen. This root may refer to the eye, the sight, the judgment, or the feeling, equally. The intuition, perhaps, is a better word than feeling. It suggests first the eye, then the appearance to the eye. If the eye, then what the eye sees. If the appearance to the eye, then the appearance itself which is reflected in the eye of the beholder.

Furthermore, from the definition Eye, follows the reflection in the eye. Then the sparkling, glittering, the gleaming appearance of an eye. Even the weeping of an eye. And so finally to what looks like this, therefore of a fountain or spring. In the latter case *ayin* refers to the eye-like gleam of water at the bottom of a dark shaft; the reflected orb of water in the depths of a well.

As to the translation 'Pool'—where water appears on the surface—this rendering is because nothing is more conspicuous in wild places than the shining eye of a tarn glistening in the bracken, a pool of water set like a blue jewel in the rocks. Lit by the sun it is so striking to the eye even from vast distances: hence the natural adaptation of the Hebrew word.

So then this word *ayin* is the root of the word *mayan* used for 'wells' in Isaiah 12:3. And, I repeat, the root itself is likewise translated into the same English word because 'the shining of an eye' suggests the glistening of water, especially when it is gleamingly alive 'living water'. Moreover, often the whole range of the meaning of the word is incorporated in the particular use of it, especially when that use has a spiritual significance.

3. Consider the Hebrew word 'maqor': translated 'well' in the Authorized Bible

Quite apart from abundant evidence in the words *mayan* and *ayin* we may see plainly from the next word introduced—*maqor*—that the concept of 'wells' is used figuratively in holy writ. As from *beer* and *bor*, equally from *mayan* and *ayin*, so now from *maqor*.

I do not mention this Hebrew as though to impress you with a show of learning, though I trust that we shall not be found ignorant: 'I would not have you to be ignorant, brethren.' On the other hand may we be kept from that infatuation with bare facts, and that pursuit of accumulated biblical data which merely feeds the knowing pride: 'Knowledge puffeth up.' But I elucidate these words in order to achieve a proper discrimination and to demonstrate how wide is the range of truth in respect of the wells of salvation.

From the following it will be seen how pertinent is the observation that this word is used as a metaphor. Psalm 36 uses the word *maqor* figuratively when it is declared in the ninth verse: 'With thee is the *fountain* of life.' Furthermore Jeremiah 17:13 reads, 'The LORD, the *fountain* of living waters.' As a final instance, Zechariah witnesses to the point in question in the thirteenth chapter of his prophecy: 'In that day there shall be a *fountain* opened to the house of David and to the inhabitants of Jerusalem for sin and for uncleanness.'

Out of the eighteen times *maqor* occurs, only thrice is it translated 'well' or 'wellspring'. Yet undoubtedly this is a proper proportion, for strictly the meaning conveyed is that of the *fountain* uncovered at its source. It conveys the idea—to use another metaphor—of the root of things. And they that are rightly instructed in the use of the wells of salvation will get at the heart of the matter when, Zechariah 12:10, 'They shall look upon me whom they have pierced, and they shall mourn for him, as one mourneth for his only son'. That is the source.

This piercing took place 'in that day' referred to by the prophet. This is the day when Moses struck Christ the Rock with the legal rod, whilst God poured out his righteous ire on the substitute of sinners. In the very same day, spiritually, a *fountain* was opened to the house of David and to the inhabitants of Jerusalem for sin and for uncleanness. Zechariah 13:1,

'In that day.' Or to view the fulfilment, 'But one of the soldiers with a spear pierced his side, and forthwith came there out blood *and water*', John 19:34.

They shall look on him whom they have pierced. Yes, but I do not believe one gets anything near a right view of the cross unless one goes to look as in the eye of one's God. Saith Jehovah, 'They shall look upon *me* whom they have pierced.' Get to the fountain of life, and gain a sight of the eternal God made flesh. See the qualities, attributes, characteristics, the nature of the Deity—in Father, Son, and Holy Ghost—then you will see the cross, and not until. This is the law of the wise, and says the wise man, it is a *fountain* of life, and so is the fear of the LORD.

The word *maqor* refers to the spring, the original fountain, the source. It really goes back to the beginning of the flow in its original purity, you see. It traces things, even fountains, right back to the beginning. *The source*. This is the law of the wise: he traces to 'that which was from the beginning.'

The wise will have none of these tributaries, much less the muddied streams that time carries from pure beginnings: no, to the *spring* he goes, and it is to him a *fountain of life*. He directs his hearers away from what has come in since the beginning, back to that very beginning itself. And to those who take heed a most sweet discovery is made: 'The mouth of a righteous man is a well—*maqor*—of life.'

4. Consider the way in which 'Wells' are used figuratively for gospel truths in Holy Writ

But time fails and time past must suffice us to have enlarged upon the Wells of Salvation from the translation of the Hebrew words for 'well'. For I judge that it is sufficiently established that 'well' is used in a figurative way of gospel truths. Not of legal truths, mind, though there are legal truths. The law is holy and just and good, but no man shall find a well by it, only a bitter death by it. Only emaciation and dehydration.

I say, by the law there is scorching dearth. Though the law be spiritual and require holy works, the man it addresses is not and has nothing to bring forth suited to it. But the gospel is life-giving; it requires no works whatever, but freely ministers grace to the hearer. The gospel is a fountain whereby a free and gracious salvation is opened unto the poor lost sinner. It is that from which wells of salvation are discovered, so that joyfully the wondering soul draws the water of life, and not only so, but they 'shall never thirst'. This is the sweetest of all experiences open to man.

These wells of spiritual refreshment in dry places were revealed in the gospel which was—by type and figure—before preached unto Abraham. It was of these that the seer prophesied in Isaiah 12:3. And so it came to pass in the fulness of time that the water of everlasting life in the Holy Ghost was plenteously forthcoming from the gospel wells of salvation.

It is clear that by these spiritual wells revealed to Abraham is meant the doctrine of the apostles to the early church. Then what deep roots are to be seen in this gospel. And no wonder: it is the everlasting gospel concerning the eternal Son of God. Everything, absolutely everything that has come in since is but cheap, frivolous substitution. For it is plain to see that by the wells of salvation the prophet refers to those peculiar, dis-tinctive, and unique gospel truths which were uncovered by revelation to the patriarch at the very first.

And moreover no more or other truths were to be uncovered or discovered at the last. What was to be revealed in the new testament the apostles fully taught, not by types or figures of the true, but in the substance of them, by the true doctrine. However no *more* 'wells' were or are ever to be uncovered than those already prefigured in the gospel preached at the first to Abraham.

You may take every single new testament doctrine back to Abraham and in form or in figure you will find it there, without exception. We have not followed cunningly devised fables, you know. I don't preach novelties, but stand in the genuine ancient tradition and old ways of the gospel, stretching away back to the patriarchs. I shall not be moved! Neither shall you be that are established with us upon this one foundation of the word of the truth of the gospel.

In fine, by the expression 'The Wells of Salvation' the prophet Isaiah refers us to the wells dug by Abraham, Isaac, and Jacob. But since they are 'of salvation' these literal wells of the patriarchs in turn point us to the *saving gospel truths* revealed unto the fathers at the first. All this is perfectly clear in and from the holy scriptures.

The good Shepherd ever leads his sheep back to the word of God. Green pastures are not elsewhere set forth. Then I say, at the direction given to faith by that word, it is to the still waters from the wells of salvation that he leads the flock actually to drink for themselves. And a true and spiritual people of God in their own generation have ever been led back to the wells of salvation and have found these spritual wells still valid for faith now to draw water therefrom: they are *the source.*

And I tell you that any minister, book, or movement that directs us back merely to some great preacher, or period, or reformation, or revival, or that harps constantly upon some of those in church history, who perhaps, may well have drawn water from the wells of salvation:—well, I tell you plainly of this 'evangelical' canonizing of saints, of this sprinkling Protestant holy water on church history, it will bring no water of life whatsoever. You merely read it once or twice if you must: BUT GET TO THE WORD OF GOD FOR YOURSELF.

Any other direction to your soul, it is not of God. No others, not even the very writers of holy writ, are wells of salvation! God complains of our day, 'They have forsaken ME the fountain of living waters.' But a man that seeks salvation does not want to know about another man that obtained it, he wants to know about IT. HE CRAVES DRINK FOR HIMSELF. *He is dying of thirst.*

Such gasping souls, on being led by the Spirit to drink from the wells of salvation, plainly see by experience what God revealed to Abraham. They give glory to God because they draw water for themselves from the wells of salvation with joy unspeakable and full of glory. They speak of the God of their salvation, and whilst they are grateful to God for taking up Abraham and revealing these things to him, it is not the patriarch they name when they make the discovery, neither is it his name that is on their lips, but the name of *THE GOD OF THEIR SALVATION.*

Therefore I think it is plainly seen and proved and shown from the use of the word 'wells' that the Wells of Salvation refer to gospel truths given and revealed to Abraham, Isaac, and Jacob, before the law was given. *Gospel* truths.

May the Lord bless the word. Hallelujah!

THE FOURTH ADDRESS

The Fourth Address

> By faith Abraham, when he was called to go out into a place which he should after receive for an inheritance, obeyed; and he went out, not knowing whither he went. By faith he sojourned in the land of promise, as in a strange country, dwelling in tabernacles with Isaac and Jacob, the heirs with him of the same promise: for he looked for a city which hath foundations, whose builder and maker is God.
>
> *Hebrews 11:8-10.*

1. The Ancient Wells of Salvation Opened in the New Testament

JUST what does the prophet Isaiah mean by the expression 'The Wells of Salvation'? Already I have shown that this refers to gospel truth. Not to all the truths found in the bible indiscriminately, mind, for the bible contains a manifold and vast revelation ranging from creation to redemption. It covers the exposition of the two testaments, and in particular their respective unfolding over several dispensations.

The bible records the history of that people to whom those covenants applied, and besides this there are many prophecies of things to come both in this world and in the next. So I say, not the bible in a general way, much less both covenants in a confused mixture. Rather it is the new covenant, the gospel, to which 'The Wells of Salvation' point in the most explicit and exclusive manner.

Indeed, men will get nothing of the water of life out of the old covenant; the law provides no wells of salvation. The wells of salvation are gospel truths which were dug—that is, opened up—before the prophecy of Isaiah but which stand good to the end of time. It is through these gospel openings that the Spirit flows. The 'wells of salvation' answer to those saving truths which were discovered in the very beginning of Israel as a people of God.

Of course the expression 'wells of salvation' actually takes origin from parallels drawn between the literal wells dug and the spiritual experiences undergone by the patriarchs Abraham, Isaac, and Jacob. The ancient fathers wandered about through a desert land and, finding no water to drink, they dug wells. In many instances the discovery of these wells was more or less synonymous with the spiritual openings which God revealed to the patriarchs in a way of salvation.

In any event, coincident or not, there was the obvious parallel of the life-saving relief from drought by the finding of water in the desert, and the soul-saving comfort of spiritual truths revealed to the heart thirsting after God.

I would point out that the word 'wells' is in the plural. The number indicates super-abundant supply for continuous need. This in itself gives the lie to the frivolous innovation which supposes that salvation is something so trivial that it may be fully communicated by one decision. As if so great a matter could be totally conveyed with but one tiny sip. Let men try and sustain the whole of their natural lives—provide for a life-time's thirst—on only one sip of water at infancy, and see how they get along.

Abraham and his seed dug not one well but one after another: a clear token that they kept on getting into fresh circumstances where—since their enemies were ever increasing and always active—they were now brought under a new necessity of being saved from the immediate menace presently confronting them. Present enemies demand present salvation, and present troubles require very present help in time of trouble. Old deliverances are of no avail then.

So I conclude that the plurality of the wells indicates the abundant provision of God our Saviour for the whole of life and every possible variety of need ever to be encountered during this lifetime. Moreover such abundance gives assurance of reservoirs of divine supply laid up in store for us in and through death, extending to the resurrection and everlasting glory of the believer: *wells* of salvation.

In fine, it is clear that the wells stand in those openings into evangelical truth exposed and revealed to the patriarchs from which flowed the waters of the Spirit into their inmost souls. The flowing of these life-giving streams welled up as by the gospel preached before unto Abraham.

Furthermore we have seen that there are in fact five Hebrew words in the old testament separately used to convey this concept of 'wells'. We have in measure glanced at those words and seen enough of their meaning sufficiently to have the truth opened up to our minds and I hope to have engaged our hearts.

Now I proceed to observe that those same wells—in Genesis—were in fact typical of the spiritual wells from which the disciples, the apostles, and the new testament saints all drew the water of life in their own experience. The fulfilment of the ancient prophecy is therefore illustrated many times over in actual consummation through the epistles of Peter, John, Paul, and the other inspired evangelical writers.

Especially is this true of the epistle to the Hebrews. There one finds many relevant instances demonstrating the spiritual refreshment of the saints in their pilgrimage through this present world. In other words of their drawing water with joy from the wells of salvation. Indeed the eleventh chapter of the epistle deals specifically with the example set by the patriarchs to the new testament saints. It is a chapter which clearly illustrates that the superior faith of the fathers translated the merely physical and material incidents of their lives into what was divine, spiritual, and eternal.

Doubtless the epistle to the Hebrews cites Abraham as the pre-eminent example of the faithful fathers. It is shown clearly that the patriarch drew with joyful faith through precious gospel truths the flowing water of life. Look what 'wells of salvation' are opened up in Hebrews 11:8-10: 'By faith Abraham, when he was called to go out into a place which he should after receive for an inheritance, obeyed; and he went out, not knowing whither he went. By faith he sojourned in the land of promise, as in a strange country, dwelling in tabernacles with Isaac and Jacob, the heirs with him of the same promise: for he looked for a city which hath foundations, whose builder and maker is God.'

I would draw your attention to the singular manner in which the writer distinguishes the lofty spiritual issues which dominated Abraham's life. With lucid clarity he perceives and unerringly points to the ancient wells of salvation from which Abraham himself drew the secret of his strength. Here, evidently, is one who discerns the very springs and motives of Abraham's life. With inspired intuition he is 'looking unto Abraham his father' so as inwardly to understand the patriarch.

And not Abraham only, for, verse 11, 'Through faith also Sara herself received strength to conceive seed, and was delivered of a child when she was past age, because she judged him faithful who had promised.' So that as well as to Abraham his father, the writer is 'looking unto Sarah that bare him'.

The author of the epistle is earnestly—and I may say fruitfully—'looking unto the rock whence he was hewn, and to the hole of the pit whence he was digged.' In a word, therefore, he is discerning the ancient wells of salvation. What shall we say that he has found?

2. Abraham's CALLING: Election and the Oath

Hebrews 11:8 reads: 'By faith Abraham, when he was called to go out into a place ...' Oh, I tell you these waters shall refresh the saints, for this passage reveals both the election and the oath of God. Observe: Abraham was *called*. God called Abraham. Abraham didn't call God. Abraham was called alone, says the scripture, and blessed. If so, both the choice of whom to call, and the intention to bless the chosen, preceded the act of calling. God *knew* whom he would call. 'God called *Abraham*.'

Election, then, for God was precedent: *he* called. The oath, for God swore blessing on Abraham irrevocably; this he confirmed with an oath. When God took Abraham's salvation in hand and blessed him, that was a springing well to Abraham. All his springs were in God. He would take neither honour nor reward from the world. No, not even so much as a shoe-latchet would he take from the kings of the earth. Abraham looked afar off to the promise of God alone, 'I am thy shield, and thy exceeding great reward'. And so it was.

It was God who took in hand Abraham's salvation. I want you to get hold of that. Because one finds that instinctively the natural intellect indignantly repudiates the truth of election. No doctrine is more likely to bring out the enmity, the wrath, the anger, the bitter hatred of men against God than the truth of election. If God is like that, saith the natural man, I will not worship him. How such men delight to misconstrue the truth and to misrepresent God.

But I tell you that to the saints, to poor lost sinners, to those who cannot move themselves or help themselves, those who feel and have been taught the truth of their natural depravity, to them election is a wonderful consolation. It is a springing well of comfortable doctrine, they love to hear that Abraham was called alone and blessed. O what a precious truth to their souls: Election and the oath, how precious, they cry. What the world most despises is what most comforts them.

The saints see that salvation is—and *must* be—all of God. As an old man of some seventy-five years Abram was well settled in the far country, and there he would have been till the day he died. *But God* appeared to him, and *God* took him, and *God* said unto him, 'Get thee out of thy country, and from thy kindred, and from thy father's house, unto a land that I will show thee.' So it was that God brought him to the land, and there it was that God revealed the spring of his eternal love to Abraham, saying with an oath, 'Blessing I will bless thee, and multiplying I will multiply thee'.

God sware by himself. He took eternity to record, brought perpetuity to witness, and took to his testimony everlasting verity, crying, 'By myself have I sworn'. This was Abraham making his decision? I tell you this: if you do not know the inward preciousness of that wonderful, wonderful saving doctrine of election and the oath then you know nothing yet as you ought to know, and the truth is that you will discover the dry pit of self-justification utterly to fail you at the last.

Free Grace was the well from which the apostles drank, and this they found amply confirmed in father Abraham. God called himself the God of Abraham. But whom do foolish men suppose came first, God or Abraham? I say, by faith Abraham, when he was *called*. Get the water out. *When* he was called. Oh, what a precious springing well.

Sovereign grace is not to us a thing of dry contention, it is something which is so sweet, so absolutely essential to our souls. We know it is useless that works of any kind should initiate from us. This is no theory. This is no cold academic notion. It is an experimental, an utterly essential heart-warming comfort and consolation to poor helpless sinners. You want to discover this well. What a precious truth. When Abraham was *called.*

So I say there is this great well for you to discover and it is ELECTION. This goes right through your bible. There *is* an elect seed. God *is* the God of Abraham and the God of Isaac and the God of Jacob. The God of the living. Not the God of the dead. Rather—as Isaac abundantly displays—he is the God who begat the elect seed *from* the dead. God is not the god of this world. For this is a world alive to man and dead towards God. God is the God of Abraham. He was a man who was alive towards God and dead towards this world.

Now you will say to me, But Abraham was the one through whom all the nations of the earth should be blest. Yes, and despite that the nations so consistently renounced the melting overtures of the love of God, still God so loved the world that he gave his only begotten Son, that the world through him might be saved. Yet him they crucified. Notwithstanding all this, the blessing of God in Abraham is such that multitudes out of all nations were, are, and shall be called by grace alone and blessed with faithful Abraham.

The elect seed of Abraham does not rectify the world. Rather their faith reproves the world, whilst their voices earnestly cry to men with the overtones of eternity to depart this city of destruction and flee from the wrath to come.

For the truth is that—so incorrigible is human nature—that this fleeting world cannot be improved. Moreover the cross was not given to improve the world but rather to redeem men from out of the world. The cross is not for this world, do you understand? It is for the world to come. Listen to the apostle Paul: 'God forbid that I should glory, save in the cross of our

Lord Jesus Christ, by whom the world is crucified unto me, and I unto the world.'

That is the way of blessing and there is no other way. Then let us pass the time of our sojourning here in fear, not in worldly conformity. Abraham did not conform to this world or its multitudes. He was called *alone* and blessed.

By faith Abraham when he was called to go out into a place which he should after receive for an inheritance, obeyed: he did not know where he was going and he did not understand how to get there. But he believed God, and it was counted to him for righteousness.

God called; by faith Abraham obeyed. You see then how that his faith followed *after* his calling. Then neither faith, nor any cause for that calling, was in Abraham. Nothing was in Abraham. All the precedent causes were in God. But those who trust in the dead letter put their 'faith' before God's calling; in fact they hardly talk of calling at all, which is not surprising for they hear no voice. With their lips they may profess to call upon God—but to his very heart God called on Abraham. The former is a dry pit of human presumption, but the latter is a springing well of divine salvation.

The former answers to the empty cistern in which Joseph's brethren thrust him and left him to die. But why? Because Joseph received fresh revelation from God, saw the heavenly vision, and delighted in life-giving communion with the love of God. Of these sweet favours the dry hardened brethren knew nothing, and in bitter jealousy they thrust Joseph into the dry pit. Now the latter—the springing well of God's calling voice—agrees with the place where the God of all grace raised up the chosen seed and blessed him, saying, 'Joseph is a fruitful bough, even a fruitful bough by a well'. Which latter is a well of salvation.

Now, to summarize what has been observed: It was when Abraham was oblivious to God that he was awakened by the divine voice. Therefore it follows that he was called *as a result of* an eternal election. We have seen that from this two things emerge: Election and Calling. Not to mention the Fall indicated by Abraham's dead condition towards God. And here is yet a third point: faith is not precedent, but subsequent to calling. Yet another thing we have seen is this: since Abraham was called to be blessed, then from eternity God determined on his blessing, and confirmed it with an Oath; 'Surely blessing I will bless thee'.

But my point at present is this—he was called. By name. In a living voice. Do you follow? Ah, here is a well. There is a lot of water down here I tell you, more than you can drink and more than I can swim in.

'Calling' is a vocal activity. It is not a question of reading print but of hearing sound. Audibly, one is summoned. A voice is sounded through the breath of a living person. 'My sheep hear my voice, and they follow me.' A voice comes by vital breath, it is the breath of life sounding through the distinct intonation and speech peculiar to that person to whom the voice belongs. Abraham heard a voice. I don't say externally, in the sense of being audible to the ears; rather it was internally in the sense of being breathed upon the soul. None the less it is applicable to say, 'He that hath an ear, let him hear what the Spirit saith'. For, whatever, he heard a voice: 'ABRAHAM!'

That is a calling. That is infinitely more than merely resting on, copying, or following one's bible. That is vastly beyond even the deepest study of the scriptures. It is an infinity of divinity above men determining to work out—or up—a biblical pattern, isn't it? 'When he was *called*.' He did not read of it in holy writ and then copy it. This voice called out of heaven to his soul, and *God* spake to him.

3. Abraham's OBEDIENCE: 'He went out, not knowing whither he went'

Now observe the mode of obedience: Abraham obeyed God's voice and went forth literally and physically. Now strictly it is not the Christian religion which is being enacted here with Abraham, rather, it is a *figure* of it. The principles of the Christian religion are being enacted in Abraham's life in a figure. To be obsessed with the *figure* of the true, and *not the true itself* is all too common an error, but it is still error for all of that.

Professing Christians are obsessed today with being led from one point or occupation to another. Just as they are enamoured of social welfare to better this present world. So glibly they affirm: the Lord led me to do this; the Lord led me to do that; the Lord led me here; the Lord led me there. Rarely in the new testament is it considered significant for the people of God as such to be led geographically from one place to another. Much less to be enamoured of anything short of eternal salvation for the world to come.

What is considered to be the vital and significant guidance in the new testament is that of the Holy Spirit in his leading the brethren together into *all truth.* When brought as one into the truth—and believe me that takes a few years—then if need be the providence of God will open up here or there or whatever. And that will be found in connection with the preaching of the word and the gathering of God's people.

But this obsession with being led from one occupation or place to another is in fact substitution for being led by the Spirit into the true, the interior, the experimental knowledge of Christ. You say, Well, Abraham went out. Yes, Abraham went out not knowing the way whither he went as *a figure of the saints going to glory*. Not as a figure of their going from one occupation or place to another on earth. Rather it was to depict their whole-hearted turning from the City of Destruction in this present world, in order to commence their journey to the City of God in the glory of the world to come.

'They that say such things declare plainly that they seek a country ... a better country, that is, an heavenly: *wherefore* God is not ashamed to be called their God: for he hath prepared for them a city.' This quotation shows that Abraham, the father of the faithful, set forth on what was *to him* in reality a spiritual journey; this was *depicted* by the type of his physically travelling to a literal land on earth. Mark, then, that the character of Abraham's obedience was spiritual, and that it sprang from faith.

The apostle Paul declares, 'Concerning spiritual gifts, brethren, I would not have you ignorant.' O but the dreadful ignorance of these things today makes one wonder, where *are* the brethren at all? There is absolutely no excuse for ignorance.

Nevertheless there are babes in Christ, and some of you who are only lately saved may feel that you yourselves have learned so little and you too feel, Ah, how ignorant I am. You cry, My leanness, my leanness! Well, to you I say that Abraham knew not where he was going and yet God still was called the Friend of Abraham. It was his obedience: it came of faith and it flourished in spirituality.

That is the way to true knowledge. It is not a question of knowledge first, it is a question of obedience. Obedience brings you into the path of light, and 'in thy light shall we see light'. And obedience is to do with zeal, 'the zeal of thine house hath eaten me up.' Yes, by faith Abraham. By faith Abraham when he was called to go out into a place he should afterwards receive for an inheritance obeyed, and he went out and he did not know where he was going, but he went. You can trust God, you know. He went alone—and so can you.

4. Abraham's SOJOURNING: His Pilgrimage with his Heirs through the Land of Promise

Hebrews 11:9 continues, 'By faith he sojourned in the land of promise, as in a strange country, dwelling in tabernacles with Isaac and Jacob, the heirs with him of the same promise.' The land of promise *a strange country*? No permanent city but rather temporary tents in *the land of promise*? What does this mean?

Abraham was some seventy-five years old when first he arrived in the promised land. Far from inheriting it, he became a mere transient. Years passed. The pilgrim life went on. Round went the wheels of time. Would he never inherit? Eighty-five years old, ninety, ninety-five years, and so far from a familiar it proved an alien country. 'He sojourned in the land of promise, as in a strange country.'

During these years, Abraham's son Isaac was born. But still the patriarch was no nearer inheriting the land. Eventually Isaac reached forty years of age. It might well be thought depressing for the patriarch—still waiting for his own inheritance—being looked upon as testator by his middle-aged heir. For by now the ancient father was practically in the grave. Isaac at forty years old was even farther from inheritance than Abraham. Finally matters became even worse: for in turn Isaac also had a son who grew to some fifteen years of age, and *still* none of them had any prospect of inheriting the land.

By faith all three heirs—from some fifteen years through to some one hundred and seventy-five years old—sojourned in a strange land in a tent. The first thing one does when one gets one's own land is to build a house, not put up a tent. One only pitches a tent when one cannot stay and when one has to move on. Gypsies! He was a nomad, three generations of gypsies and the ancient patriarch still had not a foot in the land but must needs buy a little plot with cash to provide a grave for his wife.

'By faith he sojourned in the land of promise, as in a strange country.' A *strange country*. Already he had come to it in his spiritual progress that this land was but a figure of the true. This was not his rest; there remained therefore a rest for the seed of Abraham.

Because to him this apparent inheritance was a strange country: clearly he had deduced that this land but depicted his *true* inheritance. It could do no more. Why? Because the true inheritance stood in the resurrection and was of the world to come. For *this* Abraham looked, as for a better country, that is, an heavenly.

Already he saw the land of Canaan as the form and not the substance of what was promised to him unconditionally: it was a strange country, it was typical of the actual country promised to Abraham and to his seed for ever. It was a shadow of the substance. Then what was the reality of which that land was a form? I say, That reality is the world to come, of which we speak.

What Abraham *saw* in the land was the promise that he should inherit the world, as Paul the apostle clearly interprets for us in Romans 4:13. 'For the promise, that he should be the heir of the world, was not to Abraham, or to his seed, through the law, but through the righteousness of faith.' Now nowhere does it say in the Genesis account that Abraham was promised the *world*. But I say it was what Abraham *saw* in the land of promise. This, all the spiritual perceive: 'And I saw a new heaven and a new earth: for the first heaven and the first earth were passed away.'

Then what actually happened to the three patient heirs? 'These all *died in faith*, not having received the promises.' Then their faith must have concerned the resurrection. For if they expected to inherit the promises—since they never *did* inherit them in this life—it *must* be after death.

If so, then they believed in the resurrection of the body to their dying gasp, and with their last expiring breath they affirmed faith in a new heaven and a new earth in the everlasting glory. And therefore it follows of course that they were pilgrims and strangers in the earth, for they perceived that *none* of the promises were for this life, this body, or this present evil world. All were for the world to come.

5. Abraham's HOPE: 'He looked for a city'

Everything about the inheritance *must* concern the next world after the judgment, not the present world before it. Otherwise it would perish with this world. But I observe that it is an *eternal* inheritance. Therefore the heirs confessed that they were strangers and pilgrims on the earth.

'For they that say such things declare plainly that they seek a country. And truly, if they had been mindful of that country from whence they came out, they might have had opportunity to have returned. But now they desire a better country, that is, an heavenly.' That's the country, the country of the world to come, of the new heavens and the new earth. After the resurrection, after the judgment, then, then comes the inheritance which Abraham learned by experience to seek beyond Canaan the figure of the true.

A heavenly country. And what is in that country but an heavenly city? 'Wherefore God hath prepared for them a city', Hebrews 11:16. As to this holy city, new Jerusalem, Jerusalem above, this was that upon which Abraham set his eye during the whole of his earthly pilgrimage: 'For he looked for a city which hath foundations, whose builder and maker is God', Hebrews 11:10.

Abraham dwelt in a tent in this world and he looked for a city in the world to come. He dwelt in a strange land that was a figure of his inheritance and he looked for a heavenly country that will be the reality of that inheritance.

(i) The work involved in preparing a city

It may be said, How can one possibly look for an heavenly city? Oh, you haven't got much water out of this well if you must complain of invisibility. I pray you read again: 'He looked for a city which hath foundations, whose builder and maker is God.' Here are three moral dimensions. Now, can you see anything?

Observe. The city for which Abraham *looked* had to have foundations; it must needs be fashioned through a builder; and perforce, it must possess a maker. To Abraham the realization of the absolute necessity of these three things, and the fact that God would do them, was a well of salvation to his soul. It is one of the chief of all the wells of salvation.

There is a work to be done in the quarrying, hewing, and fashioning of the 'stones' that constitute the city of God. Then there is another work to be done in bringing those 'stones' up to mount Zion and knitting them together in one. Their being put together and made one in the unity of the house of God is a thing exceeding beautiful.

But then again the city must have foundations and perhaps this is the most important work of all, the chief among the first three. Well, I tell you, his foundations are in the holy mountains. But first let us consider briefly the meaning of 'Builder' and of 'Maker'.

The Greek word translated Builder has been used in the new testament only four times. Three times out of the four the word has been translated Craftsmen. It is obvious then that the translators preferred the connotation 'craft'.

This gives the sense of an artificer, artisan, one who carves or engraves. In our context I judge that it refers to the cutting out of the stones from the distant quarry face, the carving and shaping of them ready to be transported to the holy city.

This work answers to that seen under the direction of Solomon the son of David, when preparing to build upon mount Zion. It is said, 'And the house, when it was in building, was built of stone made ready before it was brought thither: so that there was neither hammer nor axe nor any tool of iron heard in the house, while it was in building.' The individual work done away way off in the far country was with a view to being united immediately when brought together upon mount Zion.

Just so in the work of sanctification by the Spirit. Individually poor sinners are wrought upon by God, so as to be brought to the place where they can say, 'Let *us* go into the house of the LORD'.

This was the experience of Peter. 'And when Jesus beheld him, he said, Thou art Simon the son of Jona: thou shalt be called Cephas, which is by interpretation, A stone.' Thus he could say of those previously awakened, called, and born of God: 'Ye *also*, as lively stones, are built up a spiritual house.'

This original building work of God in the soul of the sinner to bring him into Christ, is described by the word here translated 'Builder'. The doctrine shows that wonderful as is this work, it is but the preparatory means to the divine end. God's purpose is realized and his end actually achieved through the church in Christ Jesus. Have you really understood that? Experimentally?

The other word is Maker. An unusual and difficult word used but once in the whole Greek Testament. It is normally explained by the idea of 'Public Worker', and if this meaning conveys the thought of work in respect of a united Public and not isolated individuals, then it is satisfactory. The new testament conception is that of the work of God in respect of the corporate people rather than of personal sanctification.

Thus the 'public worker' or 'maker' of the City takes the individual stones transported by the 'builder'—through whom they have been hewn from the quarry and fashioned—and he then knits them together, building them up into a spiritual house, making them into an holy temple in the Lord, a house for the God and Father of our Lord Jesus Christ.

To this end God has always worked and—blessed be his holy name—he is still working. He gathers his people from the north, south, east, and west, and brings the solitary into families. 'They wandered in the wilderness in a solitary way; they found no city to dwell in ... he led them forth by the right way, that they might go to a city of habitation.' To this very day, although hidden, God's unmistakable work continues: he gathers his people into the unity of the Spirit. For there is one body and one Spirit, and there is one hope of our calling. One Lord, one faith, one baptism. And there is one God and Father of all, who ever leads his people into the one unity of the body of Christ.

(ii) The truth involved in founding that city

But to return to the first of the three moral dimensions of the city of God. Hebrews 11:10 states: 'He looked for a city which hath foundations.' Now what constitutes the foundation of this city for which Abraham looked, whose builder and maker is God? What is the meaning? To answer this, permit me to show you Abraham looking for a city.

The first thing Abraham did on arrival in the promised land is recorded in Genesis 12:7, 'There builded he an altar unto the LORD'. Thus it was that, so early, Abraham showed his realization of the only foundation upon which God could establish a community—build a city—'there builded he *an altar*'.

And observe but one verse after, 'He removed from thence unto a mountain ... and *there* he builded an altar ...', verse 8. That is the second altar. The third altar Abraham built is seen in Genesis 13:18: 'Then Abram removed his tent, and came and dwelt in the plain of Mamre, which is in Hebron, and built there an altar unto the LORD.' You see how that Abraham has this deep concern—the Philistines would call it an obsession—with the conception of an altar: he built altars. Why is this?

The reason is that Abraham, from the very beginning of his experience, perceived that the altar alone would suffice to provide that sacrificial basis without which God could have nothing to do with sinful man. Because a foundation of material stones is of no concern to God. Abraham saw that. God requires a foundation of justified righteousness, he demands a *moral* foundation in which sin is judged, outraged justice appeased, and divine wrath propitiated.

Then God can build with men in mercy consistent with judgment: because *then*—at and on such a foundation—'Mercy and truth are met together; righteousness and peace have kissed each other.' Hence the foundation of God must be one in which two things otherwise irreconcilable—the sin of man and the righteousness of God—have met together in a bloody and substitutionary sacrifice. This happened at the Altar. That is what Abraham saw, and that is why he 'looked for a city which hath foundations, whose builder and maker is God'.

This sight has captivated the spiritual vision and enraptured the pilgrim heart from the beginning of the world: Genesis 8:20, 'Noah builded an altar.' This signifying in figure that the world to come after the floods of judgment would be established upon that foundation. Therefore as soon as Noah removed from the ark he gave expression and substance to his faith by building a place of sacrifice.

All the days of his pilgrimage Noah looked for a city founded upon an altar; as opposed to the men of this world, to the nations who considered such a provision totally superfluous not to mention impractical. For in the judgment of this world Noah was not 'practical'. Although no doubt there were great changes of heart when the Flood came and 'took them all away'.

Prior to the Flood of course, Noah was thought the fool and it was the philosopher whom the world considered wise. And so today men look to the world-improvement theorists of the welfare state: namely the ideologists, the evolutionists, the universalists, and the conformists. But these are not interested in an altar; if they were they would not look to this world, they would look to the next world, just like Abraham who 'looked for a city *which hath foundations*, whose builder and maker is God'.

(iii) The absence of the truth in the building of worldly cities

The worldly do not build their cities on the foundation of an altar; at most they do 'good' without one. Consider the establishment of worldly cities: they are based on the lust for money, power, and pleasure. They are full of avarice, ambition, and concupiscence, achieved by the systems of commerce, politics, and 'entertainment'. Oh! The name and mark of Cain is in the cities of this present world.

For the primitive example, observe Genesis 4:17: 'And Cain knew his wife; and she conceived, and bare Enoch: and he builded a city, and called the name of the city, after the name of his son, Enoch.' That is Cain for you. That's his city, the first city. It had foundations sunk in the blood of his brother better than he, and was named after his lust in memoriam.

There is another city in chapter 10:8-12. 'Cush begat Nimrod: he began to be a mighty one in the earth. He was a mighty hunter before the LORD: wherefore it is said, Even as Nimrod the mighty hunter before the LORD. And the beginning of his kingdom was Babel.' That is Babylon the Great, the foundation, fulness, and end of which appear in the great spiritual visions of Revelation chapters 17 and 18.

The origin of Babel is recorded in Genesis 11:4. 'They said, Go to, let us build us a city and a tower, whose top may reach unto heaven; and let us make us a name, lest we be scattered abroad upon the face of the whole earth.' That is their city. But there is no mention of an altar. There is no memory of the Fall. There is no recollection of the Flood. There is no enquiry for salvation. Already that is forgotten. Everything is based on what man will achieve.

In Babel there is no conviction of sin. There is no fear of the judgment of God. There is no thought of the need for atonement, no seeking for a sacrifice. And why? Because fallen man ignores the altar. Man's ambition despises the altar. Men build up civilization with every intention of doing so to the perfection of human paradise. Yet throughout the ages in which different kingdoms and systems have come and gone, one thing remains true of all men's building: it consistently ignores every divine principle and all revealed truth.

Therefore the notion of a 'Christian' West and 'Atheistic' East is nothing but a delusion. As though nations could be 'Christian', or as if cities differed one from the other in principle. The bloodiest persecutions have been between and in 'Christian' countries. Latimer and Ridley were burned alive at Oxford, England, not Peking in China. The Spanish Inquisition was 'Christian', naturally. It was a 'Bishop' of the 'Church' that incarcerated John Bunyan for years in prison, not a Commissar of the Party. London and New York, Moscow or Peking: it makes no difference; the principles are the same, and are summarized in the bible under the mystic conception of 'Babylon the Great'.

Then whatever may be the external distinctions, and despite the great differences men may profess and stress, once seen from heaven the cities of the whole world merge into one great whole of common basic principles: Babylon the Great. That is, not one of them is founded upon the altar; the altar is ignored. Contrariwise Abraham and his seed builded an altar, and—if you are able to receive the *spiritual* significance of this—dwelt in tents, not a city.

(iv) The presence of the truth in the building of the Holy City

Appropriately the city of God is mystically envisaged and described at the very conclusion of the bible. 'Come hither, I will show thee the bride, the Lamb's wife. And he carried me away in the spirit to a great and high mountain, and showed me that great city, the holy Jerusalem, descending out of heaven from God.'

The holy city is described as having a wall great and high, with twelve gates: 'and at the gates twelve angels, and names written thereon, which are the names of the twelve tribes of the children of Israel.' *Israel*, mark it. Whence you will observe that Abraham, Isaac, Jacob, and his seed obtained the city; they went in through the gates, you see, and left their names there as a memorial to the covenant-keeping God of their salvation.

'On the east three gates; on the north three gates; on the south three gates; and on the west three gates.' That is, being interpreted: In thee and in thy seed shall all nations of the earth—north, south, east, and west—be blessed. The called from the four corners of the earth come in through these gates by Father, Son, and Holy Ghost; three gates in each one side. I say, thus shall the people be brought in with joy of whom it is said 'God is their Salvation'. This doth not stand in a natural Jewish seed or in Jerusalem below or in an earthly Canaan: it stands in Abraham's spiritual seed, in Jerusalem above, and in a heavenly country.

Revelation 21:14 continues this spiritual description from the vision of the city: 'The wall of the city had twelve foundations, and in them the names of the twelve apostles of the Lamb.' The 'names of the twelve apostles' stands for the apostolic doctrine of Jesus Christ and him crucified, and on this the city is founded.

That they are called the apostles 'of the *Lamb*', would indicate that their doctrine points to the 'Altar', the slaughter-place of the cross. There the Lamb of God was slain, his body broken, and his blood shed. This brings in Justification by faith with all that mighty foundation of God profoundly and immovably resting upon the person and work of Christ.

The covenant number 'twelve' indicates the whole of that people of God called by grace through the gospel into the new testament. These people are properly based upon the apostolic foundation and are marked perpetually through the age in that they continue steadfast in the apostles' doctrine and fellowship, breaking of bread and prayers, and they are those on whom the fear of God rests.

'And he that talked with me had a golden reed to measure the city, and the gates thereof, and the wall thereof. And the city lieth foursquare, and the length is as large as the breadth: and he measured the city with the reed.' In the golden measure of that divine Man every issue has been faced foursquare. Nothing has been covered up, all is in the light, all measures up to 'the measure of the stature of the fulness of Christ'.

The saints have not avoided any moral, spiritual, biblical, gospel, legal, doctrinal, or ecclesiastical issue. They have not avoided the offence of the cross lest 'they should suffer persecution for the cross of Christ'. No; they have faced it all, they have faced it every way, and they have faced it foursquare and threefold and measured it up to the reed. That is the kind of citizen you find there: gold like glass. Straight as a die.

Continues the sixteenth verse of this last but one chapter of the last book in the bible—that to which all has been leading—'He measured the city with the reed, twelve thousand furlongs. The length and the breadth and the height of it are equal.' It is a covenant city as the numeral twelve indicates.

As to twelve *thousand*: ten by ten by ten—the round figure indicating completeness—points to the complete work of Father, Son, and Holy Ghost. The dimensions of volume and substance are seen also. This answers to the length and breadth and depth and height of the love of Christ, and so to being filled with all the fulness of God.

'And he measured the wall thereof, an hundred and forty and four cubits, according to the measure of a man, that is, of the angel.' One hundred and forty-four is in fact twelve by twelve, notice. This, in the wall, proposes the safe inclusion of all the old testament—twelve tribes—and all the new testament—twelve apostles—spiritual seed of Abraham by faith. And that as measured in the light of the angelic man. Here all the saints are united in one Spirit, measured as the complement of the Lamb, and are as a bride adorned for her husband.

I put it to you that this is the city for which Abraham looked; it is the city for which the people of God have looked down through the ages. Here is a well of salvation, if ever there was one. Indeed, a pure river of water of life, clear as crystal, flows out of the throne and through the midst of the city, for its delectation and health.

This then is the heavenly city in the land that is very far off, to which Abraham journeyed. He was called alone and blessed. Abraham had no earthly object in view, he looked through death to the resurrection and the world to come. He looked for a city which hath foundations, whose builder and maker is God. What a river of water of life awaits him there.

Abraham believed, and with joy drew water from these very gospel wells of salvation, as the Hebrew epistle plainly teaches. Abraham was justified by faith over four hundred years before the law was given, with which faith he associates blessing and the promise.

What wells of salvation this reveals. Abraham sets forth the death of the only begotten Son of the Father, the Lamb of God, at mount Moriah. It is all there: Remission, Propitiation, Ransom, Reconciliation; all is foreshadowed. In a word, the grand foundation of Justification by faith is clearly and fully prefigured in Abraham.

As to the wells of Sanctification, Abraham walked by the rule of the Spirit according to the gospel. This was before the ten commandments, moral law, or legal rule were even heard of or conceived. *And* the patriarch walked in such an holy manner as to shame every legalist who perforce neither knows what he says nor whereof he affirms.

Abraham weakened not, considered not, staggered not; he believed against belief and he hoped against hope. Abraham was strong in faith, he gave glory to God, and he was fully persuaded. Abraham opened up the wells of salvation for all his spiritual posterity to discover. This he did so that to the end of time they should quench their thirst, drink to the full, and quaff abundantly at the gushing fountain thus opened. So that they should with joy draw water out of the wells of salvation world without end, Amen.

6. The Figure of the Church shown in Isaac's Bride

What a well was opened up to chosen Isaac, the man born out of the dead. Is it not so? Rebekah the bride was brought home and revealed to Isaac the man of life, and how this needs to be seen today. See what a man of life he is, what his doctrine is, who his bride is, what the church is. This is what needs to be seen today.

How many people need to see the vision of the bride, for example, from Psalm 45. They have no vision of the church whatever, none at all; even what bare facts they do profess are but the result of plagiarism, and then merely learned by rote. It is all clouds of dead dust, rising from old books. They have got no revelation whatever. And it is just as true today as ever it was: 'Where there is no vision, the people perish.'

Twelve times over and more the bride, the church, is apostolically described. With the Lord, she is named The Christ. She is the Lamb's Wife. She is revealed as the Body, the House, the Temple, the Kingdom—both of heaven and of God—the New Man, the Church, the New Jerusalem, and the Little Flock.

The Bride is also called mount Zion, she is called the City, she is called the Mystery—Oh, what wells are opened up by this. How deep calleth unto deep at the noise of thy waterspouts. How precious are thy thoughts to usward, O God, they cannot be reckoned up in order unto thee. O Israel, O house of Aaron, praise ye the Lord; ye that fear God, praise him!

Because if it is a question of the bride—with the sweet and fragrant blooming of outgoing love that this implies—then the very idea becomes obnoxious, when men merely study and ape biblical descriptions or pentecostal patterns. With hoped-for accuracy they suppose to 'form' churches, copy gifts, and mimic meetings. Disgusting!

Nothing but a revealed vision by the Holy Ghost through the Son of God, commanded from the Father above, can bring in that church which is described in the new testament. She is the chosen Bride of Isaac that the servant of Abraham found by a well. 'Behold, I stand here by the well of water. And let it come to pass, that the damsel to whom I shall say, Let down thy pitcher, I pray thee, that I may drink; and she shall say, Drink, and I will give thy camels drink also: let the same be she that thou hast appointed for thy servant Isaac.' Thus he spake, and it was so: the bride was found at the springing well.

In the Song of Solomon, speaking by the Spirit the son of David describes his bride on this wise: 'A spring shut up, a fountain sealed.' Moreover he declares in another verse that she is 'A fountain of gardens, a well of living waters, and streams from Lebanon.' A fountain! — *mayan* — the word in Isaiah 12:3 for the wells of salvation.

And it is *ayin* in the case of the bride's well in Genesis chapter 24. What a distinction this reveals between false worshippers with their dry pit and the true bride who is herself a springing fountain.

This shows plainly that what gratifies the heart of Christ is the warm spontaneous love of a people brought in by the Spirit to be his spouse. Conversely, what disgusts him is the coldly intellectual copying of this by the hard and icy-hearted legalist. It is the difference between living water and dead dust.

Now I trust that we, brethren, as Isaac, are the children of promise and therefore have proved our free-born title to drink from the well. Title is not merely by the letter of scripture, you know. For it is written—Galatians 4:22-31—that Abraham had *two* sons, the one by a bondmaid and the other by a freewoman. Two, mark it; yet both from Abraham, observe.

The bondwoman gave birth after the flesh. Her offspring prefigures those that are bondchildren of the letter: they have no life in them. This bondmaid, Hagar, stood for the covenant which gendereth to bondage: this was that law given at mount Sinai in Arabia. This legal bondage of the bondchildren answers to the 'Jerusalem' which now is, and is in bondage with her children.

Oh, how these children, with all their intellectual working, all their claims for scripture, all their striving for and debating over the letter, how they love to bring the free-born sons into bondage. I say, how they fill the church with clamour and dominate it even unto this day. But these are certainly not the free-born children of promise, and no subjection should be rendered to them, no, not for an hour.

For there is an utter and complete opposite to that Jerusalem which now is. But first let it be clearly understood that 'Jerusalem below' is not in itself the literal city of that name in Israel. Rather it is a *composite picture* of the total effect—whether old or new testament—when man lays hold of the things of God and the divine order of religion, and fully takes it over.

Presently, it is visible Christendom. Today, that is 'Jerusalem below', with all the many forms of her visible and organized worldly systems of religion, which she loudly justifies by her presumptuous claims to the dead letter. Multitudes are deceived by this. For example, how many of these bondchildren, loudly crying, 'Calvinist, Calvinist' from their heads, in fact are far greater will-workers in their hearts, than all the Arminians, whom they condemn, put together and multiplied.

However in total contrast to this, the 'Jerusalem' which is above is heavenly and spiritual. Of the celestial city, Sarah the freewoman became the figure. She is viewed as the mother of all the children of promise, children full of life, born anew out of heaven from God and united in One Spirit. This heavenly and divine free birth agrees with the new testament, the ministration of which is not in the letter but in the Spirit, standing as it does in righteousness and life.

Moreover, as then he that was born after the flesh persecuted him that was born after the Spirit, even so it is now, Galatians 4:29. It has not changed one whit, and neither shall it to the end of time. By this you can tell of what sort a man may be:

whether of the flesh—despite all the biblical and doctrinal claims—or whether of the Spirit. What a well! What a well!

Then there is Jacob, too. What wells were dug by Jacob. 'Jacob have I loved, but Esau have I hated.' Jacob stood for the second Man, the final Adam, the Lord from heaven, the life-giving Spirit. The well of salvation. Jacob was the one of whose God it was said in Acts 7:46, 'David found favour before God, and desired to find a tabernacle for the *God of Jacob*. But Solomon built him an house.'

It is true that David found a tabernacle for the God of Jacob, but it was through his son, Solomon, that it was raised. Now this signifies that the house of God is built up through sonship. But then why does it state that David 'desired to find a tabernacle for the God of *Jacob*'? Why not of *David*?

Because Jacob, later named Israel, was *the* patriarch through whom many sons were raised up to father Abraham. And because Isaac, himself, was raised from the dead in a figure, *before* he begat the children of Israel. The type signifying that the house of God, raised up by a future seed of Abraham in justifying righteousness, would stand in sonship begotten through everlasting life beyond the reach of death.

This clearly depicts that the true Son of David, Christ Jesus—now raised from the dead and ascended on high—by the Spirit quickens the children of God into life. He unites them together as lively stones, building them up into a spiritual house for an habitation of God through the Spirit. By actually and really gathering the children of God together in one, in each several locality, the Son of God thus constitutes a house for the dwelling of God and the Father.

Thus the Son of David brings many sons to glory. By the Spirit, in the midst of the church, he sings praises unto God. Have you heard his song thrilling through the hearts of his gathered assembly? O! What a well of salvation. O! To feel him look up to heaven in Spirit, as in the midst of the brethren, and say, 'Behold I and the children which God hath given me'.

To prefigure this consummate reality, David desired to find a tabernacle for the God of Jacob. 'O house of Jacob' says the scripture. That is not bricks and mortar, it is the living children of Israel. For Jacob was so prolific, he was so fertile, his twelve sons were called the Children of Israel, they magnified greatly. 'And Israel journeyed, and spread his tent.'

Behold then the tabernacle for Israel's God: it is many sons. See it also in Solomon. But it is not the figure, the shadow, that is significant; it is the substantial reality. It is what these recurring and expressive figures convey that is to command our attention. And what is this but sonship? That we should be gathered into, and express, the household of faith. What a well of salvation that we should be called the children of God in Christ Jesus.

Therefore I say to you that the house of God, the church, the habitation for the God of Jacob, is built up by birth. But not natural birth. As says the psalmist, in spirit contrasting the cities of this world with heavenly Zion, 'This man was born *there*'. This profound well of salvation was enacted with Jacob at the ford Jabbok, where there wrestled a heavenly man with him till the break of day. Jacob called the name of the place Peniel: 'I have seen God face to face.' What a figure of regeneration.

Jacob's name was changed, his nature was changed, his natural strength was broken, he obtained the blessing, and beheld his God. This is the experience of regeneration. All night he wrestled. With the strength born of sheer exhausted desperation, with the sheen of sweat from hours of grappling with his God wet upon his pallid brow, Jacob gasped, 'I will not let thee go, except thou bless me'. That is the experience of being born anew. Have you been to Jabbok's ford? What a well it is.

But time fails me in multiplying examples of the wells of salvation, now revealed in the gospel. I have taken several instances of spiritual wells from which Abraham drew, as they are expounded in the new testament. I have lightly touched upon one or two examples of this with Isaac and Jacob. I have been careful to revere holy writ and to submit to those principles governing its spiritual interpretation. God is witness: conscience bears record: I have not shunned to declare unto you the whole counsel of God.

Give ear, O ye heavens; and hear, O earth, the words of my mouth. My doctrine shall drop as the rain, my speech shall distil as the dew, as the small rain upon the tender herb, and as the showers upon the grass:

Because I have published the name of the LORD: ascribe ye greatness unto our God.

He is the Rock, his work is perfect: for all his ways are judgment: a God of truth and without iniquity, just and right is he.

THE FIFTH ADDRESS

The Fifth Address

> And in that day thou shalt say, O LORD, I will praise thee: though thou wast angry with me, thine anger is turned away, and thou comfortedst me. Behold, God is my salvation; I will trust, and not be afraid: for the LORD JEHOVAH is my strength and my song; he also is become my salvation. Therefore with joy shall ye draw water out of the wells of salvation.
>
> *Isaiah 12:1-3.*

1. The Spiritual Means by which Water is Drawn from the Wells of Salvation

FOR the last four addresses you have been directed to the wells of salvation in and of themselves. Now I intend to show how water was and is to be drawn from these wells thus located. Therefore this fifth chapter is devoted to considering the spiritual means by which the water of life is freely obtained from the heavenly wells.

And it is by spiritual means. For we know that it is neither with cord, rope, chain, nor yet is it with bucket, bottle, or goatskin, but it is with heavenly joy that the divine and living water is drawn. And moreover we know that there is but one source whence it is obtained, namely, from the gospel wells of free and saving grace in Christ Jesus.

How important this is. For just as surely as Nadab and Abihu procured strange fire from a forbidden source obnoxious to God, so there are multitudes today who fulfil this type by claiming to have the Holy Ghost, yet in reality possess nothing but overheated passions ignited by alien flames and fanned by false spirits. Not from the Wells of Salvation, but from strange waters they draw: from forbidden outlets and weird sources.

However I tell you that the true and living waters of the Holy Ghost derive from one source only: it is the glorious Lord Jesus Christ declared according to sound doctrine. By this the gospel wells of salvation yield abundantly to heavenly experimental joy in Christ. How agreeable to the word of God! But anything else whatever must be from another spirit, another Jesus, and another gospel. And anyone advocating anything else must be of the false apostles, deceitful workers, and no minister of the gospel at all.

This divine exclusiveness is what the inspired psalmist found. God would not share his glory with another. The waters of the Holy Ghost were not to be drawn up by a rope of works, neither by bucketfuls of free will. No, nor by the strength of man's arm. David discovered that to draw water from the wells of salvation, nothing but joy, heavenly joy, would suffice.

This water of life would come up by no other means, no, though one deepen the vessel, lengthen the cord, strive to lower the whole by self-righteous works of the law, or labour to raise it again by the arm of the flesh under the gospel. Though one cast in never so many old devotional books, push over veritable volumes on divinity, sink down whole theological libraries, all thrown into the shaft from the top to raise the level at the bottom, nothing ever did rise up and nothing ever will come up, but by joy.

Hence David said, Restore unto me the joy of thy salvation. He saw that it was all of God. It was by free grace alone. Only

God could restore David, and give to him the Spirit's joyful witness of restoration. Then with joy he should draw spiritual water from the wells of salvation. 'Restore unto me the joy of thy salvation; and uphold me with thy free Spirit.'

But to return to our text. Isaiah 12:3 does not mean that when one draws water by some unspecified means or another *then* one is to do so joyfully. No: *joy itself* is the actual specified means by which water is to be drawn up from the wells of salvation. As to the use of joy in the drawing of water, this has been wonderfully prefigured and typified by the children of Israel in a number of general instances. However, in my judgment the most striking single case is that to which I now draw your attention: it is recorded in Numbers 21:16-18.

'And from thence they went to Beer: that is the well whereof the LORD spake unto Moses, Gather the people together, and I will give them water. Then Israel sang this song, Spring up, O well; sing ye unto it: the princes digged the well, the nobles of the people digged it, by the direction of the lawgiver, with their staves. And from the wilderness they went to Mattanah.'

In the first place I would like you to notice how this certain well is located: 'And from thence they went to Beer.' Yet this is not as definite as it sounds. Because as you are aware—or should be by now, in view of my having taken the five Hebrew words translated Well—'*Beer' means* 'well' in Hebrew. It is not a place-name at all. It is the name of a thing that is at a given place. In fact the name of the place is not mentioned.

By transliterating the Hebrew, and giving the word a capital 'B', the translators have made the word look as though it were a place-name. It sounds like the Hebrew or Arabic name for that location, but it is not, it is simply the untranslated word for 'Well'. And that is all.

In fact three words further on in verse 16 the word *beer* occurs again. And this time, arbitrarily and inexplicably, it *is* translated. 'And from thence they went to Beer: that is the *well*.' The only difference here between the word *Beer* and the word 'well' being that in the first case the word has been left in the Hebrew, whereas in the second place, quite rightly, the Hebrew word has been translated into *well*. Of course it should read, 'And from thence they went to the well; that is the well ...'

The point which emerges from the correct translation is this: the very fact of the omission of the proper place-name deliberately *suggests* a spiritual location, a point reached in the soul's journey, a moral place. This cannot be reached by geography, and nobody can locate this 'well' cartographically. No, and no more are they intended to do so. A fact incidentally true of all these biblical locations which the superstitious and ignorant so promptly idolize, draping them with embroidered rags and hanging bits of gilded metal and carved wood all around, turning them into 'shrines' at which they grovel.

I say therefore, that the lack of translation is a grievous omission. The *transliteration* 'Beer' naturally suggests a place-name to the English reader and this gives the exact opposite to the desired effect. In fact the Hebrew text by its very vagueness insinuates that this well is to *figure* as a spiritual place, not to be reached by physical means.

In a passage inexplicable were it not figurative, it is obvious that the physical and geographical facts are deliberately glossed over in order to show the insertion of typical and spiritual verities into an otherwise bare historical narrative. Thus is conveyed a figure of what is discovered at this point by the saints upon the journey of faith to the rest that remains for the people of God.

2. The Lessons Learned by the Children of Israel in their Journey to the Well

But now I want to go back a little into the previous context. The first words of verse 16 indicate the wisdom of this: 'And from *thence* they went to Beer.' From whence? Follow back to verse 13, 'From *thence* they removed.' Again in verse 12, 'From *thence* they removed.' Notice verse 11, 'And they journeyed *from*.' Once more in verse 10, 'And the children of Israel *set forward*.'

You see there is a question of great eagerness to get to this place, and swift progress from one stage to another. Previously, the lessons of each single stage had taken at least a chapter—sometimes several chapters—to recount. But not now. Here the narrative runs through five stages in a mere six verses. In fact the whole chapter covers as many as ten stages. Urgency. From *thence*, you see, runs back so swiftly that it is hard to tell exactly whence.

Consider then the experiences they must have had 'from thence'. What spiritual exercises, what swift and vital progress made together in the way. They had proved God as their Saviour and they had proved that they were his own peculiar people. They had proved it, I say, experimentally and unitedly. Thus it was that they came to the Well and were enabled to demonstrate in a figure how with joy to draw water from the wells of salvation.

To speak of that place from whence they came to the Well therefore involves that one should recount the lessons and experiences of Israel in the wilderness up to this stage. For the very running together of the narrative—the mere fact of the swift progress—would seem to suggest previous long and slow disciplines now well learned. Then 'from thence' would indicate from *having really imbibed the lessons of the wilderness by suffering experience.*

Therefore I say 'from thence' would involve summarizing all the journeys of the children of Israel up to this moment. It would incorporate all the lessons learned to bring them to this place at which they had arrived. It would include all that had made them hardened spiritual warriors full of ingrained experience. It meant that they had graduated from the school of God in the wilderness by hard discipline and deep soul humiliations.

(i) The war with King Arad

To illustrate this in the context of Numbers 21, observe that the first verse tells how Israel came from being beaten by the enemy. 'When King Arad the Canaanite, which dwelt in the south, heard tell that Israel came by the way of the spies; then he fought against Israel, and took some of them prisoners.'

The heathen idolaters took some of *them* prisoners? Oh, tell it not in Gath, lest the daughters of the Philistines rejoice. What? Israel came from being thrashed by their enemies? But 'When Israel went out of Egypt ... The sea saw it, and fled: Jordan was driven back. The mountains skipped like rams, and the little hills like lambs ... Tremble, thou earth, at the presence of the Lord.' But *now* where was the mighty God of Jacob?

However after this chastening lesson Israel came from thence, penitent and heart-broken, thus to gain the victory. For, having been so miserably defeated, the consequent humiliation gave rise to such a spirit in them which would God were in the people today, 'And Israel vowed a vow unto the LORD, and said, If thou wilt indeed deliver this people into my hand, then I will utterly destroy their cities. And the LORD hearkened to the voice of Israel.'

But today where is this spirit against the spiritual enemies and the doctrinal enemies that have swamped the true people of God, overcome the congregation of the righteous, and captured some of us? Tell me, where is this spirit? For once it was true of us that: 'Ye sorrowed after a godly sort, what carefulness it wrought in you, yea, what clearing of yourselves, yea, what indignation, yea, what fear, yea, what vehement desire, yea, what zeal, yea, what revenge!'

(ii) The people were discouraged by the way

Consequently, Israel came on from having utterly destroyed the enemy. But then, after all that, they got discouraged by the way. Oh, publish it not in the streets of Askelon; lest the daughters of the uncircumcised triumph. They got discouraged by the way. Which way? Numbers 21:4, 'And they journeyed from mount Hor by the way of the Red Sea, to compass the land of Edom.' Now Edom is Esau their brother, he who sold his heavenly birthright for a mess of earthly pottage.

Ah, well, this is the old way of the natural discouraging the spiritual as they pass by: here is all the discouragement from fleshly relations. All their hatred and envy when one of their brethren and number, now born again of God, wholly serves the Lord. 'As then he that was born after the flesh persecuted him that was born after the Spirit, even so it is now.'

This is the way in which: 'I was a reproach among all mine enemies, but especially among my neighbours, and a fear to mine acquaintance: they that did see me without fled from me.' Moreover: 'My lovers and my friends stand aloof ... and my kinsmen stand afar off.' And again, 'Thy mother and thy brethren *without* seek for thee.' Why not *within*? And the soul of the people was much discouraged. Because in this way a man's foes *shall* be they of his own household, not satisfied till the saints are altogether made like the world again.

So Israel betook themselves to fault-finding with everyone and everything except the true cause: their own weak stomach for spiritual separation through a clean testimony. They did not murmur against Esau or themselves. Oh, no. They murmured against God and against Moses saying, 'Wherefore have ye brought us up out of Egypt to die in the wilderness?'. And the people spake against the heavenly manna and the spiritual drink crying: 'Our soul loatheth this light bread', 'neither is there any water.'

Over-familiarity with the wondrous signs of God in the midst and blasé nonchalance at continuous miraculous providence caused them to ascribe it all to mere natural causes. Encouraged by worldly brethren, they murmur against God and his servant Moses; they despise their heavenly lot and spurn their spiritual portion.

'And the LORD sent fiery serpents among the people, and they bit the people; and much people of Israel died.'

(iii) The brazen serpent

Ah, yes, to the Well they came, but with many gaps in their ranks, and empty places in the tents. For they came from having been plagued with fiery serpents which slew the brethren in vast numbers. They came from seeing mounds of the dead in Israel rotting under the sun, slain by the wrath of God, judged by the outraged Holy One in the midst of them.

They came from seeing the brazen serpent lifted up on a pole in the wilderness. 'Even so', saith the scripture, 'must the Son of man be lifted up.' It was not—God forbid—a brazen figure of the Son of man, mark, but the brass figure of a serpent. The type, then, stands in the lifting up: not in any remote resemblance between the appearance of the two things lifted up.

This—Numbers 21:8—is far from being the simple type so often supposed by the unspiritual and ignorant. Indeed it is one of the most difficult of all the types to interpret correctly in the whole of the old testament. More often than not it seems to be badly, and sometimes to be appallingly, handled. What then is the significance of the raised brass effigy of the serpent?

In the brazen figure the vicious origin of sin is seen at its very source: not man, but the serpent. That is what is judged. Not the venom injected into mankind; nor even the venom of itself; the serpent *himself* is judged. Judged, because brass is the metal of the altar: it is the basic substance of the place of judgment.

Just as the brazen altar is the symbol of the place of divine justice, so brass becomes the figure of that justice in itself. Sin is judged by God at its absolute genesis; God's judgment is seen as dealing with the embodiment, the origin, the root of all the evil that ever came into the world. And if so, then before man fell: for the serpent in all his malicious evil approached man when in his innocence.

Then the type of the brazen serpent is not dealing with symptoms; it is not dealing with the individual person affected; it is not even dealing with fallen man as such. The figure is not one of the judgment of man in Adam by whom sin *entered* into the world. What is being depicted by this type is the judgment of God on the serpent as such. It is judgment of evil *before* it entered into the world by man at all.

It is the satanic embodiment of Eden's serpent that is fixed in brazen condemnation. *That* is what is condemned in judgment on the pole. Now just *look* at that. The dying saw how deep the judgment went, and must go, and were healed. They saw it: no intellectual problems in Genesis to dying men. All the survivors had looked and lived.

This type is a tremendous picture of evil being judged in its original entirety, as traced back to its inception. God's judgment is seen in his utter abhorrence of all evil from the last vestige to the first trace, and even to the origin of that trace: what caused it?

Yes, you see, that is what is in view. It is not a question of some mere abstract serpent being judged, that would make the figure both impossible and ridiculous, wouldn't it? It has to be a question of what *the* serpent implied, of what he was and what he had done, and therefore was doing. *That* was the cause of any contemporary manifestation of Evil. They must see that, and judge it to the root in its totality.

Had they steadfastly trusted in God they would have been kept from the Evil. Despite it was no more they that did it but sin that dwelt in them. But where had that come from? Satan. When? With what effect on the race? How profound must judgment be before God could have to do with them? The brazen serpent gives the answer, and the living must really, actually, inwardly see and perceive that it is so, to live.

It is a question of seeing how total must be God's judgment of evil before his holy nature can be satisfied and approached. It is not a question of seeing Messiah but the *reason* for Messiah. It is a question of seeing what must be condemned, and how exhaustively, before God can have to do with men overtaken by the Evil One. The Israelites did not look at the Saviour, or a figure of the crucified Messiah, they looked at a figure of a *brass serpent*. They looked at a brazen figure of *Satan*.

They had to realize the *depth* of the judgment needed. From *that* lifted up to view they gained the truth as to how deeply must suffer quite Another also lifted up to view. You must see the first lifted up, to realize the *reason* for the similar lifting up of a completely different second. One was a brazen effigy of Satan the serpent; the other the actual human body of the Son of man.

The lifting up by Moses—the law—was the same; the being exposed on the pole was the same; the shocking weight of divine judgment was the same; therein stood the type. But to make the brass serpent—Satan—itself a type of the Son of man is an appalling, shocking analogy. It is a type of *what* he was lifted up to *abolish*. Jesus came to *destroy the works of the devil*.

How profoundly, how perpetually, how totally he wrought that destruction is revealed by this sight of Satan abolished and fixed rigid in eternal judgment.

Jesus did that to Satan at the cross. Did what? Look! Look! Just *see* what the cross *did* to that old serpent, called the Devil, and Satan. Get your doctrine right. Get your sense of sin and judgment right. Get your knowledge of the cross right. See how and where the prince of this world was judged. To see Jesus' victory, *one must see why*: and equally, over *what*. *Then* one can see *in whom*.

This is one of the most thorough figures of mercy and of judgment in the old testament and of course it is from there that real progress follows. No hold-ups, no stopping at a place and learning endless lessons over and over again. From thence, they hurried forward and went every one from strength to strength toward Zion.

(iv) The progress made when the figure of the serpent was applied

Numbers chapter 21 verse 10: the children of Israel set forward; then they go on in verse 11, they journey, they pitch towards the sunrising, light is breaking; they go through in verse 12 to the valley—where the water is found—and so on and so forth, and see! there is no lack of water on their way. No lack of water.

Hence we read in verses 14 and 15: 'What he did in the Red sea, and in the brooks of Arnon, and at the stream of the brooks that goeth down ...' That's it, there is plenty of refreshment from that place where sin is seen judged at its root, when evil is condemned at its source, when there is no room for the flesh. Look and see what progress is made.

Oh yes, they came 'from thence'. They came from knowing out of trial how weak they were. They knew how backslidden they were, they had discovered that whilst at one moment they were prepared to adulate and almost idolize Moses, the next minute they were prepared to stone him with stones.

They knew now by experience the vacillation of their hearts, they knew the corruption of the flesh, they had discovered their naturally helpless bondage to Satan. They had made all this self-discovery, and so they had been brought into the light, they had been brought into the battles: they acknowledged all this, the only basis of truly glorifying Christ and his work.

Now this is what brought progress; I say, what a flow of water and what vital increase is made from really judging sin and the flesh to the root and from owning the truth of the dread eternal judgment of God. What increase from confessing the world as alien and from judging that the Canaanites are enemies, real enemies, who must be slain, and whose cities utterly destroyed.

Of course this does not mean — to us — destruction in a physical way, because in that sense we have got nothing to do with the sword or violence or suchlike things. We don't protect ourselves by force or retaliation; but what this does mean is seen in a moral way at least, as to separation and discipline in the church. There can be absolutely no room for the flesh.

First there must be self-judgment and secondly there must be judgment in the church. Doctrine must be pure; spiritual experience must be required. The Holy Ghost must be sought to assert the rights of Christ and his renown must be pre-eminent. Real progress follows, and there are no hold-ups and no learning lessons again, they hurry forward to Zion, that's the lesson they learn from there, and what progress one does see when the antitype of these things is admitted and applied.

(v) The book of the wars of the LORD

At this point there is another thing that I should mention before finally leaving the context. It is referred to *en passant* in verse 14 of chapter 21: 'Wherefore it is said in the book of the wars of the LORD.'

Then the saints fully recognized that the LORD has wars. Note that 'wars' is in the plural, that there are a sufficient number of them to make up a book. Notice with what familiarity the writer refers to this book; also how obviously he expects his readers to share this awareness. Further observe that it is the mind of the Spirit that the record should be written for a memorial to future generations.

Therefore whether it be material enemies in the old, or spiritual in the new testament, the instructed people of God recognize that there *are* enemies. They recognize that the enemies must be fought, that they must be beaten, and that the victory must be maintained. And from thence they came to the Well.

It is no good, my brethren, ignoring the war, avoiding the cross. It must be admitted that the friendship of the world is enmity with God. Marvel not if the world hate you. Friendship with worldly churches too, even if they appear to have real Christians in them, the position is still enmity against God; don't play the fool.

'Let them return unto thee'—saith Jehovah to Jeremiah—'but return not thou unto them.' It is no good compromising, you have to recognize that the LORD has wars and if you expect to go through war without any cuts, or slashes, or without being really hurt, or pierced, then you will be sadly disillusioned in the event.

The wars of the LORD. There are enemies and there is judgment—the people are righteously judging things. Judge your enemies and fight them; prevail in the conflict; maintain the victory; remember it; and be watchful for the next battle. That's how you get to the Well. And I tell you that you won't get there any other way.

See! How this contradicts that dreamy sentimental make-believe travesty of the Christian religion which supposes that the great goal is to be so 'nice'—in a vapid, innocuous, simpering affectation—that no one could ever possibly be offended.

This product of the modern church is called by them 'A Christ-like spirit', but in truth it is a downright offence to the Lord and his gospel. It is nothing other than: 'Peace, peace; when there is no peace.' But to them, He came not to bring peace, but a sword. Zionward to the Well! 'From thence.'

3. The Concept of the Church as a Corporate Body: 'Gather the People Together'

There is awareness of the Well. Now, this is specific. The antitype is that there is definite united recognition of the Spirit's presence—of the inward waters—below. The well is beneath: there was a reservoir of divine supply answering to the desire of Israel to rise as one body to the mutual worship of God in the Spirit.

For this there was something that was actually located in the earth; it was not something which flowed down from a source up in the mountains. It was not the waters from the 'Rock that followed them'. No, it was a question of something with a hidden presence, a reservoir, directly down here with them, the whole body of this water was invisibly there below; they recognized that.

The well, I say, is beneath; there is a mutual awareness of something coming from within the midst of the assembly. And moreover it was for all Israel, 'Great is the Holy One of Israel *in the midst of thee.*' Saith Christ, 'I will declare thy name unto my *brethren*, in the *midst of the church* will I sing praise unto thee.'

In the figure, the Well is that which sprang up in answer to united worship from the midst of the assembled congregation. The people had reached the place where the whole of Israel was seen as a separated, vigilant body, a worshipping company in an alien atmosphere, a people experienced in the school of God: this is the place of the Well.

From thence the Spirit answers that corporate body. I say, the Spirit warmly answers to their response to Christ's testimony. It was felt and experienced that by one Spirit they had been all baptized into one body, they sensed together that they had been all made to drink into one Spirit. A shout of praise was in the camp. Thus it was that the waters moved below, and the well gave forth abundantly.

And I would add that today if the people of God are to answer to these heavenly realities, if they are going to ascend up to the measure of the actualities of divine life, then two things must take place.

First, there must be an utter disdaining and rejection of all pretence. There is *so much* mimicry and pretension. So much human imitation to cover up the fact that *God* is not supporting our position. Then again—secondly—we in turn must be led of God through the equivalent spiritual steps to those taken in the figure by Israel 'from thence' in order to arrive at last at 'The Well'.

On our pilgrimage we too must recognize the enemies: but for us they are enemies of the cross; enemies of experimental gospel doctrine; enemies of what is truly spiritual; enemies of the true assembly of God's people. Certainly we are to love and forgive *our* enemies, personal animosity and retaliation being forbidden. But as to the enemies of the gospel we have to recognize them and be men of spiritual warfare.

That means therefore, since one goes to war, that there will be veritable armies against the true pilgrim people of God. Not only the world in general, but also in particular the Pharisees, Sadducees, chief priests, scribes, elders, false brethren, false prophets, false shepherds, of our own day and generation. As with the Lord and his apostles, there will be whole classes, whole sections against our spiritual progress, and not without but with their 'religion'.

'From thence they went to Beer: that is the well whereof the LORD spake unto Moses, Gather the people together, and I will give them water.' One might have thought they *were* gathered but evidently not in as coherent a way as that in which the word of God now directed. The wording is put in this way in order to emphasize the fact that they were not assembled *in relation to the well.*

You might have considered the command unnecessary and superfluous since they were not some mixed congregation of Israelites and Egyptians, as is the equivalent generally today. Much less were they the remnant of the twelve tribes scattered to the four winds, and denominated to be joined to many uncircumcised nations, as is so with the professing church in principle at this present time.

No, they were all true Israelites, pilgrims all, discriminate and separate. They were united too; *but* not yet in the most important way, not yet in a divinely corporate way, for God said after all their spiritual progress from thence, '*Gather* the people'. Oh, what a lesson this is in respect of the Holy Ghost today.

Every merely individual spiritual exercise, even the deepest exercises of salvation; every ministry, even the profoundest experimental ministry: all is to divine purpose. Hence all will come to dust unless it results in personal subjection to the discipline of being gathered mutually as one into the church. 'All ye are brethren.' That is the one, the only permanent place of grace and peace: the place where it is multiplied.

The gospel is designed to manifest the body of Christ and bring the called into the house of God; it is the gospel of God, and they who receive it are baptized by one Spirit into one body. Both professional clericalism and its attendant sectarian denominationalism of necessity negate this conception. Therefore these two enemies must be faced. It is not right to avoid these two issues. Neither is it honest.

However I cannot deny that facing such spiritual warfare will mean mortification, humiliation, and chastening. It will mean a suffering way, my dear friends, a suffering way to 'Beer'. But:

> The saints thou art uniting
> In faith, in hope, in love,
> 'Mid scenes of conflict guiding
> T'ward that bright rest above.

Gather, saith God, Gather the people together and I will give them water.

When one speaks of the Lord Jesus Christ, one speaks of the Head; and if one speaks of the Head one must envisage the Body. He is 'Head over all things to the church, Which is his body.' To speak of the Lord Jesus Christ therefore, and contentedly to fall short of being experimentally united with the saints in the Body, veritably this is to draw nigh to him with the lips when the heart is far from him.

And so with the gospel of God. If one speaks of the gospel, but in fact one pares it down to a light and worldly 'evangelistic' context, or to the confines of a sectarian denominational structure, one is in error. The *true* gospel is the *antidote* to these things. The true gospel *necessarily* takes out the world and brings in the church of God. Indeed, *given* the gospel in the true and apostolic sense, *follows* the church of absolute necessity.

Either the Spirit leads into all the truth of the one Faith or he does not. Either the Spirit is one Spirit or he is not. Either there is one God and Father or there is not. Either there is one Lord or there is not. But *if* there is then there *must* be one Body. And of course there *is* one Body. But if so, this should be visibly manifest:

> The bread reminds us we are one,
> One body there is seen;
> The Spirit's unity we own
> Where diverse we had been.

Numbers 21:16-18 sets before us the type of the Holy Spirit here below in the midst of the assembly of God's chosen people. The Spirit is typified as it were within, beneath: located bodily. This figure is seen in relation to a pilgrim people separated from the world, and from false religion. Then God says, Gather the people, and I will give them water.

And I say to you, this is what is needed: the gathering of the people in *this* way. Not simply as seen at the Passover; not merely called out from Egypt; not only viewed from the banks of the Red sea; not just envisaged from under Sinai's lowering brow; no, not even solely as gathered to and by the truth set forth in the tabernacle.

Certainly a people embodying all that truth and experience. Definitely a people who have taken up that tabernacle and gone through the wilderness carrying it on pilgrimage sustained by manna and the 'Rock that followed them'. Assuredly a people who have recognized and fought the enemy. Necessarily a people who have judged the flesh in all its workings to the very root. But more. A people who have been brought from thence to the Well. A people brought in love to become verily indwelt by the living God.

Being thus gathered, forthwith the responsive speech of God is this: 'I will give them water'. This is a promise addressed to living faith. When God first speaks these words, the water is yet underground: nothing at all can be seen by the people. The word is in the future tense and the water is by promise.

Observe then: given that the gathering takes place first, water does not even then come of itself. Rather the Well springs up in response to the mutual faith of that gathered people. They believe in the specific promise to them as found in that position. And verily their faith maketh not ashamed.

So what you will find among a real people of God as thus gathered is that there is a wholehearted response in consequence of their having gone through previous exercises. Faith has been experimentally developed and answers to promise. Straightway, at the speech of God, we see that they have no more doubt about the promise to them than they have about their self-existence.

4. 'With JOY shall ye draw water'

'Then Israel sang this song, Spring up, O well; sing ye unto it.' They believed that by singing the water would come, not by digging. And if you say, But the elders digged, I ask you, With staves? How much earth can you get up with a stick? Israel sang!

So I repeat: when God once spoke, no more than spoke, and that by promise in the future tense, *then* gathered Israel sang. Israel sang, not to the water, mark, but to the well. Not after it was dug—withal by rods—but before it was dug. Observe carefully the order. Verse 17: Israel sang; after that verse 18: the princes digged.

Not only had they faith, but more: they had no doubt whatever; it was almost past faith. I mean faith which is seen is not faith. Faith was swallowed up in sight; even as they believed, they were already rejoicing in fulfilment. And so it is, when once God's presence is powerfully felt among the assembled people.

They feel that he inhabits the praises of Israel, they feel that whoso offereth praise glorifies him. Their singing was not calculated or dependent upon certain conditions: their vivid awareness of his presence whom their soul loved made praise spontaneously to burst the gates of their lips. Nobody had to tell them to sing.

I tell you that this responsive singing indicates joy. In answer to the joyous singing the waters gurgled and laughed and gushed. So I tell you it is a demonstration to a gathered people that with joy they should draw water out of the wells of salvation: this is exactly how the waters came up. With joy! There is a spontaneity about it, 'Then was our mouth filled with laughter.' There is a joyful exuberance.

But you must realize that this deep joy is very far removed from the flippant, airy effervescence of superficial modern evangelicalism. The glossy-covered, lightweight, slick evangelism of today ignores the deep scars, the blackened sunburn, the leanness, the mortification, where all superfluous flesh has been burnt from off the true pilgrims, whose rejoicing is marked by trembling.

What a difference there is between today's worked-up fleshly excitement and that holy joy brought in by the Spirit of God. The one subsides in giggling and the other rejoices with trembling. There is no doubt about that joy which does not contradict but stands in the fear of God. Prays the Lord Jesus for the gathered disciples: 'That they might have *my* joy fulfilled in themselves.'

This gift of joy is divine in origin, heavenly in nature, spiritual in character, everlasting in duration, and of God in its very essence. No wonder that, in answer to such joy, the heavenly wells yield, the spring gives forth, and water is drawn from the wells of salvation.

There is this spontaneous outburst of song. It is not that Moses sings, you see, or that someone preached: no, Israel sang. They burst out into singing. Israel awoke in a lively and vital response at the mere mention of Jehovah's promised proposal that he would give them water.

They believed God. They did not sit down in glum silence condemning Arminian works, or despising Israelites who had fallen on the way, or enviously criticizing chosen servants more gifted than themselves. They did not lie in passive and quiescent somnolence, pretending to wait for the sovereignty of God. The fact was that they loved him. The fact was that they were alive. The fact was that they burst out with joy.

What a testimony! How they rejoiced and exploded into praise and responded to him. They did not sourly, miserably, and ponderously look at certain scriptures to see whether the pattern indicated how they should perform; no, no, no, life itself demanded this, life itself awoke a spontaneous outpouring of joy in song.

The children of Israel acknowledged the presence of water which was not otherwise manifested than by the word of God. They did not grieve the Holy One of Israel in the midst of them by unbelief. They did not grieve him by limiting him or by distrusting him, nor were they discouraged by the fact that the things they looked for were things unseen as yet.

They believed him whose presence was typified by the Springing Well. They believed God and thus it was that—hearing the joyful sound—in figure they received the water of life by the hearing of faith. They received of the well by the believing outburst of praise: that is how it happened.

This signifieth the Spirit himself in the midst of the church. He is here, he is still present, and I tell you of a truth that to a divinely disciplined and united people he answers in the same manner. In fine, then, this very type is fulfilled by the Spirit in the midst of the gathered saints.

5. Recognition of the Presence of the Holy Spirit

But one will never find this fulfilled in those who are not broken in heart and who do not tremble at his word. Mutual heart-brokenness and united contrition of spirit is in fact what the gathered saints have in common. It draws them into one with many a fervent prayer, many a trembling lip, and with many a falling tear. Their melted hearts flow together as one.

You see, the Spirit is not grieved solely by treacherous ecumenicalism. There are other causes of grief than this. He is not only quenched by erroneous ecclesiastical associations. There are far deeper and more primary reasons for his being quenched. The Spirit is not offended merely by clerical affectations. He is first and more offended in matters of one's own heart.

How many have 'come out', as they call it, but without these deeply personal and profoundly interior exercises of soul and spirit before God alone. Come out? But for no more reason than that others have done so, and thus is set a kind of self-righteous fashion: O! The Spirit is grieved with this. There is no brokenness in such people.

They are hard and brittle. They judge others but they don't judge themselves. They are unkind, unforgiving, and heartless. They judge the ecumenicalists but they themselves invent and organize feeble federations contrary to the word of God. Then they have the impertinence to thank God that they are not as other men.

But the heart-melted, soul-bruised, contrite, self-afflicted man who is of God judges himself first. The Spirit is grieved deeply with these men of hard uncircumcised hearts who are content with the dead letter, with traditional orthodoxy, with a mere exterior form, with historical postures. They know nothing of the overwhelming guilt felt at one's own unfeeling part in what now breaks one's heart because of what it had done to Christ and his Body.

But now mortification hath wrought its perfect work. A brass serpent has been reared before the eyes of the soul by revelation, and the pride of the flesh has been dealt a mortal blow. Now nothing but the Spirit will do for the poor saints.

Already they have experience of streams in the desert in a personal way, as I may so speak, and these have led them to seek together the well of the Spirit in terms of worship. 'There is a river, the streams whereof shall make glad the city of God, the holy place of the tabernacles of the most High.' So they found in their experience.

The presence of the Spirit is definitely recognized for the supply of all the saints, for the indwelling of the one Body, and for the fulfilment of unity in worship. Thus it was as if their souls flowed together into one, they flowed inwardly into each other, as in a fusion of love they were all bathed in the water of life and blended within in a fluidity of love divine.

The presence of the Spirit is emphatically recognized; now that is what I want to emphasize. This follows from such a gathering of God's people in the unity of the faith, the unity of the body, and the unity of the Spirit. It is recognized that to a gathered people, there is a manifestation of the Spirit in the meetings of the saints that can never be known in or by the saints on their own. That is what is recognized.

The Spirit takes up his residence in the Body; the congregation of the saints come together in the definite and conscious recognition of this, as I may so speak. Although invisible, in the Body he is present in person. By this I mean his actual Person is thus manifest in the body of Christ: not his gifts or his blessings, but his Person. It is in this most profound sense that he indwells the church as such. That is what the 'gathering' manifests.

What an expression of worship. It is the present justification of the past death of Christ, his seeing of the travail of his soul and being satisfied. By his death he gained for his people the Spirit: and the Spirit and the Bride say, Come. Now the justification of his death is seen, in the last analysis, in the unity of one body under his headship. So it is also that the cry, 'Abba, Father', ascends from worshipping sons from out of the House of God.

What outbursts of joy should come as the presence of the Spirit is definitely recognized. What response to the supply of the Spirit felt in the inward parts, through the whole church: thus is the Spirit shed abundantly, rising up, welling over: Waters to swim in.

The certainty of the promise of *Beer* makes the saints sing for joy: shout aloud with praise to the wells of salvation. I say, what outbursts of joy should come from those who are brought of God to *Beer*.

What flowing waters, what living springs, what spiritual issues, what a shedding forth abundantly of the Holy Ghost, in these springing wells. Israel sang! Israel sang! This is what they did as a people who had been gathered together.

Oh to hear the Son say from the midst of the congregation, '*Behold* I and the children which God hath given me', and, 'In the midst of the church will *I* sing praise unto thee'. Can you hear that song? Brethren, can you harmonize with the Chief Singer on his stringed instruments?

May God give you to feel a real and genuine spiritual exercise in answer to what has been set before you.

May God 'grant you'—not thee, alone: it is plural 'you'—'according to the riches of his glory, to be strengthened with might by his Spirit in the inner man;

'That Christ may dwell in your hearts by faith; that ye, being rooted and grounded in love,

'May be able to comprehend with all saints what is the breadth, and length, and depth, and height;

'And to know the love of Christ, which passeth knowledge, that ye might be filled with all the fulness of God.

'Now unto him that is able to do exceeding abundantly above all that we ask or think, according to the power that worketh in us,

'Unto him be glory in the church by Christ Jesus throughout all ages, world without end. Amen.'

THE SIXTH ADDRESS

The Sixth Address

Therefore with joy shall ye draw water out of the wells of salvation.

Isaiah 12:3.

HITHERTO this verse has been opened up in order. We have seen to whom the 'ye' of the text refers. We have considered the word 'therefore' and observed the reason for the drawing of water. The wells, too, have been located and defined. So has the water itself. We have enquired, How then is this water to be drawn? The answer has been returned with ringing conviction and with a witness, 'With joy shall ye draw'.

Throughout, the question has been asked and answered, What is the nature of the wells? Of what are they constituted? Salvation is the answer. They are the wells of salvation. Many other things may be true of these wells, but none is truly comparable with this one thing: salvation. Certain other factors may be predicated of all the wells, and certainly there are facts peculiar to each one. Notwithstanding, one great common denominator stands out and towers over everything else: they are wells of *salvation*.

The very word 'salvation' rings with joyfulness. It is resonant with jubilation. The carillon of salvation peals throughout the new testament. This is what is paramount in the gospel. It is *the* sound that distinguishes the church. Salvation is pre-eminent. The very name of 'Jesus' embodies salvation. He came into the world to save sinners, and he effected that salvation for multitudes before he left it. This is the final word of our text. Let the LORD have the last word, my brethren, my sisters: it is 'Salvation', it is paramount, and it is nearer than when we first believed.

No wonder, then, that with joy Israel drew water from the wells of salvation. In the nature of the wells, how could it be otherwise? 'Israel sang.' We cannot be amazed that outbursts of joy welled forth from those who were brought of God to *BEER*. It had to follow: 'Then believed they his words; they sang his praise.'

Divine satisfaction ensues. The responsive love of God is shed abroad amidst the saints. See the manifestation of Jehovah's pleasure in the sweet psalms and songs of his people. What flowing waters, what living springs, what spiritual issues, what abundance welled forth in answering love as 'Israel sang'. Now then, that the Lord our God may bring us this blessing also, let us observe *how* they sang, who thus with joy drew water from the wells of salvation:

'And from thence they went to Beer: that is the well whereof the LORD spake unto Moses, Gather the people together, and I will give them water. Then Israel sang this song, Spring up, O well; sing ye unto it: the princes digged the well, the nobles of the people digged it, by the direction of the lawgiver, with their staves. And from the wilderness they went to Mattanah', Numbers 21:16-18.

1. The Singing

Actually, there are as many as six different Hebrew words for the act of singing. This indicates the great development of the people in the praises of God. Not least of the six is *Halal*: 'to boast, glory, praise'. From which, of course, the famous Hallel.

Moses and the children of Israel referred to the LORD himself as their song. Saith Job, God is my Maker, who giveth songs in the night. Much of the prophets is in verse. David was the sweet psalmist of Israel; his son wrote one thousand and five songs, and crowned this with 'the song of songs, which is Solomon's'.

Many of the psalms were written to music, some for a particular instrument, and all were arranged for vocal melody. Certain of the psalms were dedicated to the priestly singing of the Levites. And what shall we say of the Chief Musician? I will say this: he who would understand these things must discern the mind of the Spirit: not as repeating forms, but rather tracing the figures of the true.

However, in Numbers 21:17 the Hebrew word for 'singing'—then Israel *sang*—is *Anah*: 'to answer, to respond'. It is therefore a responsive song. It has an object which calls forth this outburst of praise. It springs of gratitude, it is the welling joy at being so closely cared for, so intimately cherished by Jehovah, as is now so evident by the display of his love. O! What a response this calls for: *Anah* is the word; then Israel 'responded'.

This is the word in the one hundred and forty-seventh psalm. 'Sing — *anah* — unto the LORD with thanksgiving.' You see something has been given, thanks is due. But the kind of thanksgiving the psalmist calls for from Israel is the singing known as *Anah*. He does not want the pompous, formal note of duly paid vows, barely whispered through politely restrained lips, gloved hand dutifully patting back a stifled yawn: God forbid! The full-throated roar of spontaneous praise is united Israel's lively response.

Moreover, if there are some six different words for the act of singing, including our song of response *anah*, then it need not surprise us to discover that there are up to five separate forms of *Anah*. These five forms range from that which has been translated 'Oh; O ...' through 'Lament' to the general 'Answer', used two hundred and thirty-four times, arriving finally at 'Sing' in our text of praise.

As you may easily deduce, the reason for these five separate facets of the one word lies in the wide variety of the dealings of God with his people—from chastisement to consolation—calling forth a correspondingly varied form of response.

What response! Then Israel sang. Sang in answer to the real presence of the Spirit below, springing within. The Spirit's voice as it were symphonious with that of the bride, sweetly harmonizing in dulcet counterpoint. The well rose; flowing, bubbling, rising with the swelling response to Jehovah who gave this water: 'I will give them water.' And so it was, and Israel sang to the well.

Israel sang this song, 'Spring up, O well; sing ye unto it.' An unusual song? But then none but a chosen generation, a royal priesthood, an holy nation, a peculiar people, ever reach this place and are enabled by experience to sing the rare melody. They are that little flock, that despised 'sect everywhere spoken against' who alone 'show forth the praises of him who hath called them out of darkness into his marvellous light.' They were once not a people. But, believe me, they are now a people, and that of God.

An unusual song? But then, there are at least seven different Hebrew words for song. Just as there were some six for the act of singing, so seven words for the fact of song. If *this* song is unusual, it is only unusual to us because so few in our time reach the place and begin to sing.

O! how much have we to learn of spiritual praise, of singing in and by the Holy Ghost. To take the case in point, my brethren; neither natural flair, nor singular talent, much less cultivated expertise would do for this melody at the Well. It comes of mutual spiritual life, this singing. It derives from sound doctrine experimentally inwrought. It is 'I will sing with the spirit, and I will sing with the understanding also.'

Some seven Hebrew words for song. Then what a developed people in praise, response, and lament. And no wonder if 'Whoso offereth praise glorifieth me', and 'Thou inhabitest the praises of Israel.'

The Hebrew word used for song in our text is '*shirah*' and it occurs but thirteen times in the whole bible. It is used for the title of Psalm 18, A song of deliverance. It describes the song of Moses at the Red sea, and David's song of deliverance also. But then again it occurs as the title of Isaiah's song to the wellbeloved concerning his vineyard.

The point which I would convey from this is that even within the compass of the one word, *shirah*, the range is extraordinary. What a variety is seen in the laments and melodies given by the Holy Ghost to the people of God.

What a gift for all seasons! No wonder we are instructed to 'admonish one another in psalms and hymns and spiritual songs.' This implies not only the considerable diversity of kinds of singing but also the large scope of the type of song. And if so, then the vast range of spiritual experience for the heart to express.

'Spring up, O well; sing ye unto it.' This is the song of all Israel, is it not? This is Israel's song-answer: Then Israel sang, answered, responded—*anah*—with this song, *shirah*. It is a song of deliverance from the world, the flesh, and the devil. It is a song of gratitude: Israel had been brought by the Wellbeloved into the realm of the Spirit: to the watered vineyard of Jehovah: unto the well whereof he spake, 'Gather the people together, and I will give them water'.

2. The Song

In the English bible the responsive song opens with the words 'Spring up'. But in fact there is only one Hebrew word, *Alah*. It is the word used for Ascension. It occurs in Psalm 24:3, where the question is asked, 'Who shall *ascend* into the hill of the LORD?'. The answer is given by a description of the perfections of the Son of man. After this, first the resurrection then the glorious ascension of the Lord Jesus are seen. But the triumphant entry of the Lord, the King of glory, is consequent upon his having been mighty in battle. And where but on earth? And for whom but his people? Then, then he ascends and enters through the everlasting gates.

Alah is also used for the Ascension in Psalm 68. This is quoted by the apostle Paul in his letter to the church at Ephesus: 'When he ascended up on high, he led captivity captive, and gave gifts unto men.' Without doubt this points to the ascension, seating, and reigning of the Lord Jesus, as a result of which the redeemed church below receives and is filled with the Holy Ghost from above: gifts unto men. No wonder 'Israel sang' in anticipation, and we are 'lost in wonder, love, and praise' in consequence.

Also *alah* is the word that is used for 'burnt offering'. The word neither means burnt nor offering: the word is *alah*, which means to ascend; it is not even an ascending offering, it is an Ascending. This was the main offering for the children of Israel, it was the offering of acceptance.

Acceptance might be based upon but it did not stand in a sacrifice below; it stood in an Ascension above. The acceptance in heaven of that which had been sacrificed on earth gave witness of reception not by men but by God. Peace with God, Romans 5:1, is in consequence of having been justified by faith. We have peace with God through our Lord Jesus Christ: that is his *ascended* title.

Alah is the word, I say, for ascension. It is therefore faith's song-answer to free grace from a people who see themselves ascended to God in Christ, accepted in the Beloved. By faith they see themselves seated in Christ on high. It is a calm, holy, believing response to the full glory of this same Jesus, now made both Lord and Christ. This glorious ascension brought down the Holy Ghost and that is what brings up the springing well: in turn this is what calls forth the church of the living God. To this vision of the Son mutual faith responds. 'Spring-up', to ascend, is Israel's song-answer; and 'Spring-up' is the word for the Ascension.

This song is the response of a whole people. You don't get a person seen in answer to the ascension, you get a people seen in answer to the ascension. Grace unto you and peace from God our Father and the Lord Jesus Christ is the apostolic greeting to the church as such. The 'you' is plural, and is seen in connection with the ascended title. The ascension is a well of truth setting forth the saints' united acceptance as seated in heavenly places in Christ Jesus, having been justified by faith.

Imputed righteousness is the foundation of the apostle Paul's doctrine in Romans and the basis of that in Ephesians. It is marvellous to observe the clarity with which Paul perceived the truth in Christ for all saints. Yet so much of this deep insight of the great apostle was owing to those many years of preparation spent staring down into the wells of Abraham. Indeed the epistle to the Romans might be summarized as a radiant exposition of 'Abraham believed God, and it was counted unto him for righteousness'.

The apostle Paul sees the saints' acceptance in heaven above as being founded upon their justification at the cross below. '*Being* justified by faith, we *have* peace with God through our Lord Jesus Christ.' The Son of God is viewed as seated in the glory bearing the scars of wounds incurred through effectively putting away his people's sins whilst still on earth. Therefore, given the Ascension, both he — the Surety — and they must be accepted, at rest before the face of the Father.

And as the saints praise and believe this precious uncovering of the word of Christ, so the Spirit below answers to the ascension above and bursts forth within the midst of the gathered saints in praise to that grace. How the well springs up in accord. How the Spirit meets the bride to glorify Christ ascended and to say, Even so, come, Lord Jesus.

'Ascend, O well.' This song desires the Spirit to trace up from below, the full heights of the Son's ascension above. It calls for the Spirit's answer to the ascension in the midst of a people singing faith's response to that doctrinal well. This is, I say, the well opened in Ephesians. Not just an answer in the church to the resurrection, the epistle reaches to the full heights of all that Christ has brought in for the saints, and into which the Holy Ghost would conduct them. Even beyond the resurrection it is 'I ascend unto my Father, and your Father; and to my God, and your God', John 20:17.

And now that Christ is ascended, now that the Spirit has been given, the Father seeks for worshippers to joy in believing response to this glorious Ascension. The Son cries on high to his God and Father: 'I will declare thy name unto my brethren, in the midst of the church will I sing praise unto thee', Hebrews 2:12. In answer to the spiritual voice of the ascended Christ sounding in the church below we respond, 'Spring up—*alah*—O well; sing ye unto it'.

And make no mistake about it, that is why the Spirit is given: he has come to glorify Christ amidst the united saints below. The Spirit came from the Ascension, as John 7:39 teaches, 'The Holy Ghost was not yet given; because that Jesus was not yet glorified.' But now he *is* glorified, because he *is* ascended, and so the Holy Ghost *has* been given.

As given, the Spirit of truth has come to glorify the ascended Christ and speak of him: and that within the saints below as gathered to the unity of the body. I say, the Spirit was given when Christ was glorified. He came from the ascension and therefore the descent of the Spirit answers in the saints to the ascent of the Son. That is what the Spirit would bring into the church.

Yes, even in the type of Numbers 21 the saints, discerning acceptance before the Most High, shout with joy at the grace given unto them: singing unto it. Sing ye unto it, then. Observe they are telling *themselves* in song to sing unto the well, even whilst they are singing unto *it*, itself, to spring up. And that you must do, speaking to *yourselves* in psalms and hymns and spiritual songs, singing with grace in your hearts to *the Lord*.

And so they came to the Well: 'Then Israel sang this song, Spring up, O well; sing ye unto it: the princes digged the well, the nobles of the people digged it, by the direction of the law-giver, with their staves.'

Now observe that as the people sang this song, so both the princes and the nobles digged. But with what? And at whose direction? And who are these persons? What and whom do they signify? Let us now attend to these questions.

Notice that the people as such do not expose the well, they sing unto it; the well is uncovered for them by their nobility. These notables are named in the eighteenth verse. Three ranks are seen: the princes, the nobles, and the lawgiver. Three activities follow: digging; again, digging; and the giving of direction. As regards the twofold digging, one rather unlikely kind of implement is used, namely: staves.

3. The Labourers

(i) Firstly, Princes

These are heads, or captains of the people. These notables are governors and they are appointed and they would speak of a proper order amongst the people of God. They are chosen officers marked out by appointment and speak of an external authority according to the word of God. This excludes all unchecked enthusiasts and separatists, and wholly repudiates disorder in the assembly of God's people.

The correspondence with this in the new testament can be seen in the Acts and the epistles. Within the apostles' fellowship and in the discipline of the church there was an order established to prevent the lawlessness of the flesh from asserting itself, either in doctrine, worship, fellowship, or the ordinances. Such a church government vigilantly denounces every form of disorder.

The apostle Paul in his absence instructs Timothy by letter as to the conduct that became the minister of the gospel in the house of God, the church of the living God, the pillar and ground of the truth. What were these instructions which Timothy was to obey? They concerned the prayers of men, the dress and behaviour of women, the relative position in the church of men as opposed to women, and moreover the exclusiveness of the ministry to men alone.

Furthermore, Timothy was to submit meekly to the authority of God vested in the apostolic word, and attend to the appointment of servants or deacons, of overseers or bishops—a plurality of office, not ministry, within one church, notice; no authority exists for one 'bishop' over several churches—and finally in like manner the appointment of elders also. It is not in the minister's competence to ignore, alter, abrogate, or delegate this divine charge.

In consequence, the brethren were to accept the proper administration of the divine order as given in love by the duly obedient minister of the gospel. Such an appointment must be well-deliberated and well-tried; it would indicate suited persons, consistent with those descriptions given for all to read and compare in the word of God.

Those men of God who were called and raised up of the Lord, whose fruitfulness bore record that they had a ministry sent down from heaven, those who were well known by their labours amongst the churches, it was to these preachers that this work fell.

In other words, churches had been raised up, saints were united, believers were edified, and souls saved under their ministry. The apostolic charge to them—within those churches under their pastoral labours—was that they were to appoint proper persons for the care of souls. All this was and is consistent with scripture.

The saints were to accept this appointment provided only that it was seen to be agreeable with that same word of God to which the ministers of the gospel themselves must be subject just as much as each and all the brethren.

Therefore this external order of necessity upholds unity, repudiates rebellion and disorder, and declares against those who can tolerate nothing in authority over themselves. That is, it is clean contrary to those people who can stand no discipline, restraint, government, or appointment in the church at all, but must for this reason rather leave it and set up their own lawless and impertinent inventions.

Furthermore this discipline of the one house of God harmonizes perfectly with the full liberty of the Spirit amongst the saints and in the church. For it is imperative that the spontaneous expression of the Spirit amongst the brethren be carefully safeguarded and cherished.

If a man has some measure of gift and has somewhat to say to the people, then certainly he should say on. Of course he is to mortify the flesh in the use of that gift; naturally he must keep within his actual experience. But not so as these precautions prevent him from opening his mouth. Otherwise his fears shall overcome his faith, and we shall never have the benefit of his spiritual experience from one year's end to the other.

Furthermore, if *any* man speak, let him speak; in this, it is not a question of having a gift, a man has a right of conscience to speak in the church. Only it should be according to the oracles of God and from a spiritual conviction that this matter must be declared.

If one has a gift of the Spirit in ministry by all means one is to use it and use it freely. Save only that this use must be as of the ability which God giveth, and it must be as leaving room for others also. All things decently and in order.

Just as the ministry of Christ to the church differs from the ministry of the Spirit in the churches, so the gifts and ministry of the Spirit in the churches and the right of a brother to be heard are two distinct things. All the brethren have a right to be heard in their convictions: only that they humbly regard the due order and proper discipline.

There is external order in the church. There are those however, who can stand nothing but what is devoid of any office or appointment; they cannot stand it, they are utter levellers. Whilst professing that Christ is head of the church, they will not permit him to send his ministers to that church. Others cannot stand that the man should be head over the woman, and these also invariably fulminate against the truth that some should be appointed in office over others, particularly themselves; they absolutely hate it.

But they are utterly and completely in the wrong and they should be rebuked sharply. For I tell you, God hath set some in the church, first apostles, secondarily prophets, and so on, and besides this God has set some for government: elders, overseers, deacons, and servants in the house of God.

I know that in the broken and denominated state of the church the difficulties are staggering. But then, my brethren, Abraham staggered not. Moreover I will admit that with clericalism victorious in what is so blindly accepted as the ministry, the confusion seems dark and hopeless. But, ye children of light, Abraham hoped against hope. Finally I am aware that—with such widespread ignorance as to the nature of these offices and their present application—this presents difficulties which, on consideration, seem impossible to solve. But, my fellow-labourers, Abraham considered not. On the contrary, he was fully persuaded that what God had promised he was able also to perform. And so am I. So that notwithstanding all the difficulties princes still indicate, still hint, and still speak of a divinely appointed order for the pilgrim people of God.

The minister Titus is expressly informed by letter from the apostle that there should be elders in every city. Not some cities only; but in all those meetings where the brethren had been gathered under the apostle's preaching, there should be elders ordained. And they are ordained. And they are ordained by Titus: nobody else. And similar elders are to be ordained by such ministers as are of the spirit and doctrine of Timothy and Titus in the apostle's absence ever since.

By the apostolic description and instruction recorded in the epistles, as led therein by the Spirit, and as proven in experience, so such ordination takes place in peace, concord, and agreement. The church agrees, but does not appoint. Nor do elders appoint either themselves or each other. Order becomes the house as well as spontaneity—there are bishops, deacons, overseers, and servants—and neither are we to suppose that these things change with the ruinous apostasy of the large professing body.

To talk of the church being in ruins, if by this is meant the external professing body, is all very well. But why should we become another ruin beside it? The antidote is to depart from the ruin or apostasy and humbly and brokenly return to that order and to that house that becomes the glory of God so far as it is manifest amongst us.

And if we have not got such a ministry or such 'princes' who answer to these qualifications, well then, in humble and contrite meekness let us be still and wait upon the Lord in prayer together. As indeed—God is witness—this has been the case with many my beloved brethren, who with me these years past cried to the Lord our God in prayer-meetings day and night that we might rightly return to that which became his holy name and worship. For years many of us met daily to cry to the Lord, and this was the whole occupation of our meeting.

Princes, then, speak of order. The ascension cannot be answered to unless there is order in the house of God, the church of the living God, the pillar and ground of the truth.

(ii) Secondly, Nobles

These speak of quality rather than office; do you understand? In fact they are The Quality, though not in the worldly sense of elevated position, for as to the way of this world 'not many noble, are called'. But I mean in the spiritual sense of humble and intrinsic worth. The Nobles are The Quality—as it used to be said—although that expression has gone out of fashion now of course. They are the spiritual nobility, upright men full of spiritual rectitude.

The Hebrew word means literally, willing-hearted; liberal; freed men: and it would speak of attainment in sonship, free-born. The quality of sonship, not just the potential of it. This word 'Nobles' implies grown sons in the spiritual sense: those with the maturity of the adult. It is therefore implicit that childish things have been put away, the vanity of youth left behind.

Nobility contains breadth; it has largeness, expansiveness, there is no pettiness, no triviality. That is the Hebrew meaning. This bespeaks the character of new testament sonship and is seen in the total absence of small-mindedness, the absence of miserliness, the absence of niggardliness, the absence of meanness. That is the mark of a spiritual gentleman.

However, here we have the Nobles of the people; and if of the people then the superior from among them. Neither will the majority ever attain to quite that high degree of nobility, but all will come nearest to it when the best examples are elevated before the whole people.

The fact that there are Nobles of the people, then, far from arguing all men are equal, shows that not only are some more equal than others, but some are positively and indisputably superior to all. Where these are not the leaders and exemplars, woe to that people.

There are differences indicative of leadership, as demonstrated by the word Nobles, and if these people are not exalted you will find the ignoble soon scramble to elevate themselves. Then you will see that when the vilest of men are exalted, the wicked walk on every hand.

Yes, nobility implies the absence of greedy ambition; nobles are not 'climbers'; nobility knows no crafty schemes of self-aggrandizement or advancement, it is sincerely unselfish in the interests of that which lies under its hand. You will find that the servant that ruleth is the worst despot that you can possibly have. You want true nobility to rule. Real gentlemen are needed: genuine spiritual quality.

Of course in speaking here of the quality of nobility I am speaking of the things of God. What noblemen of poor natural birth we perceive in John Bunyan and in William Huntington for example.

Ah, but how noble was the great J.N. Darby and so many others of the early Brethren. Time would fail to speak of dear and gentle Tyndale, of Wesley and of Whitefield, of Gadsby and Philpot. Then again, Martin Luther was a noble character in church history. So was George Fox.

And there are many other outstanding people who appear to tower above the ordinary. Generous, benevolent, and altruistic, the noble is devoid of the sly conniving and devious backbiting of the ill-bred place-seeker. The old nobles of God's people were marked by their true unselfishness in the love of God and of the saints: they were genuinely disinterested, honestly self-forgetful; they cared not neither did they labour for men's opinion: they feared God and cherished souls: their devotion was both unalloyed and sacrificial, and the people recognized their quality with gratitude.

But I must hasten to take up my parable, and continue. You know now what 'Princes' indicate. You know what is intended by 'Nobles'. The prince is the outward office to which the inward quality of nobility corresponds. Would God that many shall be found among God's people with this precious and noble quality, that we may all be inspired by their example, and that princes may once again reign amongst us.

But now let us turn to consider the labour of both princes and nobles respectively.

4. The Labour

(i) Firstly, princely digging

The first time the word 'dig' occurs in our text, it is in connection with the labour of the princes. The word is *Chaphar*, and I have good reason for telling you this. The word *chaphar* means to dig into a thing, to get to the bottom of it. It means to search. What a need there is for the equivalent to this in the church: for princes and rulers and nobles in Israel to search for themselves.

We don't find this today, it is not there is it? It means to search, my dear brethren, and there is no reason why this activity should not be fulfilled in you in your measure. Many of you have far more advantage than I had for example. I did not open a bible until I was twenty. It was a closed book to me: I did not know that there were two testaments; indeed had I been told to fetch a bible, I would as likely have come back with a Hymn Book, a Prayer Book, or a Koran.

But once regenerate and called, the Lord taught me to dig; I never turned to man, never, never. I had and have no need to get my matter from men, or steal other men's words, or get my sermons out of books. All I have is from God alone. To the sneers of many whose names would surprise you, I turned to God and God only for my gospel, and unlike many, I know that I have got my doctrine entirely from the Lord, and exclusively from the bible.

Mind you, I hold no brief for ignorance: I am not despising sound and spiritual reading: I am despising *making intellectual browsing a substitute for the witness of the Holy Ghost, from whose inward teaching alone the minister receives his matter. Moreover I am despising the seeking of that witness from anywhere at all outside of the holy scriptures themselves*. Reading is another thing. It is to do with general awareness and proper intelligence: but *not* to do with getting the word of God for the people. And, on the subject, many currently accepted books, particularly by infidels and upholders of erroneous systems in religion, *should never be read at all*. The Spirit is as against the saints' reading them, as was the Law against the Israelite eating unclean meats.

Before God I lie not. God is witness. 'When it pleased God, who separated me from my mother's womb, and called me by his grace, to reveal his Son in me, that I might preach him among the heathen; immediately I conferred not with flesh and blood.' In evangelicalism today there is such conferring with men, such ignobility. But let them not deceive themselves that this will ever produce one single minister, because it will not. It will, with total inevitability, prevent any such production.

Can you not dig in your own measure? Indeed you can: go in this thy strength. What a need there is for everyone according to the grace given—and particularly for our princes and rulers—to search for themselves. In my experience, to dig by searching means really to give your time to getting into the matter, to get on your knees and fall on your face to find that God who seeth in secret.

It means to search by getting alone in the closet, eye to eye with God, by reading and re-reading your bible—whilst crying the meanwhile to the Lord for grace to help in time of need.

It means to be brought to the end of that awful, dreary, soul-drying, heart-breaking extremity where you feel you have got absolutely nothing and that you never will have anything and that it is impossible for you to get a word from God for yourself. When under the heavens as iron and upon an earth like brass, with strength spent in vain and the land of the soul withered and barren, one feels one will not get to a fruitful union in God even if one lived to a thousand years. When you get there in your closet then, then you will have arrived at the place where it shall be said unto you, 'Thus saith the Lord'.

But few will submit to these disciplines, they are not noble enough, you see, they are not noble enough. Mediocrity fills the high places of evangelicalism, they receive honour one from another, they esteem the things that be of men, it is a day of mean, grey, uniform, man-fearing sameness: men are afraid to stand out: But be ye not like unto them, my beloved brethren.

Don't say that this is beyond you; for it is a true saying, If a man—any man—desire the office of an overseer, he desireth a good work. This is equivalent to princes now, and their digging means getting alone in the closet as God enables, day by day, week by week, and year by year. I say according to your ability, it means getting a large place in your devotions.

The principle applies in measure to all the people as being rightly led by the princes as their exemplars. If one complains that these are lacking today, then who can tell how highly God will promote the true aspirant to the vacant office?

Sometimes it seems that you get nothing out? But you are praying and reading, my friend: there is a cry from heaven, 'Behold, he prayeth', and you are laying a good foundation for a work perhaps twenty years hence, lay it well. God will not fail you. Like Caleb you shall inherit this mountain in due time. Backbreaking work it may be the meanwhile, but it is princely digging nevertheless.

You are exhibiting already the quality for which that divine and spiritual office is given of God to men. A quality which involves digging over the great wells of doctrine. Getting down to the great truths of scripture, digging over every particle and seeing first the dampness, then the little pool, and at last the springing well.

You are getting the doctrines to open and yield; God is giving you water; soon you shall stand back and see the whole doctrine in perspective. O yes, perhaps it is over a period of several years. But then that is digging, that is searching.

That is what J.N. Darby did, you can see that straight away. He was pre-eminent, whatever men may say. And, following on, Stoney, Kelly, and many their brethren. In like manner the early Methodist preachers, men like John Nelson for example. Luther did it. So did Calvin, and a host of others. And each in his measure many an unknown simple farm-labourer has searched through his bible in the attic by candle-light; or in the side of the rick at dawn; or cried to the Lord for his fellows under the light of moon and stars.

Many a poor rustic weaver — think of the princely John Kershaw, for example—has gone off up in the coppice or down into the trench, and has wept over the bible, with the sweat standing out on his brow from the sheer effort to trace out the words. Verily I say unto you, in his way he has done as much as ever scholarly John Wycliffe did, and has shown himself a true noble in the house of God.

Why do you want to be a worm of the earth? Mount up with wings as eagles. Lie no longer among the pots; be no longer as wine upon the lees: mount up, aspire and make something out of your life above your failed fathers and your pathetic contemporaries. There will be leaders worth the name when you get this kind of digging. 'Instead of thy fathers shall be thy children, whom thou mayest make princes in all the earth', Psalm 45:16.

Dig into the wells of salvation, dig; dig out the word of God, do what those old spiritual giants did and inspire your generation as they did theirs. What they did was to become princes. I will tell you the translation into Hebrew of that English, 'Prince with God': ISRA-EL. Now then, fear not. In due season we shall reap if we faint not. When old Moses is dead and gone, then surely we shall enter the land and inherit, and verily we shall be fed. So cry now to Joshua: 'Give me this mountain.'

(ii) Secondly, noble digging

Now this is the second time that the same word 'dig' has occurred in our English text. Nevertheless in the Hebrew the second word is different altogether from that used on the first occasion. The former, in connection with the princes, was *chaphar*. Not so with the nobles—despite the deceptive uniformity of the English translation—the second time the word is *Karah*.

Karah means 'dig' in the sense of 'to prepare'. As opposed to *chaphar*, meaning dig in the sense of 'to search'. That is, search for something hidden underneath the surface: the princes did that. But the activity of the nobles is described by this different word, *karah*. To prepare. To make friable for sowing, or, make ready for something.

It is the word used in Psalm 40:6, 'Mine ears hast thou *opened*.' David speaks in the Spirit of Christ, giving prophetic utterance concerning Messiah's divinely attuned hearing. There was no blockage, no barrier, no hindrance, between the heavenly whispers of the Father in eternity, and the perfected ear of the Son in time. All the mind of the Father was conveyed to the heart of the Son because 'Mine ears hast thou opened'.

Opened so as to be prepared for the penetration of the seed of the word, so that the word will have perpetual entrance—the hearing of faith. That is noble preparation.

As to the saints, this preparation means being made ready by the Spirit to receive the voice of Christ, to be taught of the Spirit in the wells of salvation, to have the word dug into one, to experience what it does. Thus one is prepared by spiritual and experimental acquaintance with the Divine Spirit, for the voice of the Eternal Son, as bringing one to the knowledge of God and the Father.

This preparation would involve all the experience on the way 'from thence' to the wells of salvation. All the prior work of the Spirit. They digged this for themselves, they had got it, it was their experience and it made them noble. Thus it was that they could penetrate the surface and open it up for others.

They knew the sound of the alarm, had felt the plague within their own hearts, had been thoroughly awakened to eternity, knew the converting power of God, they had seen a sight of the crucified Lamb, they knew the sanctification of the Spirit, knew the anointing, the earnest, the sealing of the Holy Ghost: all this and more they dug in their experience.

And where is that today? This is what makes a minister, not some petty, trivial, paper qualification. This is the quality that justifies the appointment of an elder, an overseer, a deacon. How many today can give such an account of the work of the Spirit in their souls? Aspire to this, my brethren beloved and longed for, call upon the name of the Lord for it, make your prayer and supplication therefore.

Nobles change generations, they set men aflame for God, they change history. Aspire to dig experimentally; who knows what God may do? Dare to be singular. The nobles exposed the wells, because they were spiritually prepared and the delighted Israel sings not to them but to it, and the waters flow from the wells of salvation as thus drawn with joy.

(iii) The use of staves

Dig with a staff? Much you will lift. A staff is not suited even to cut turf or sod, let alone to lift heavy clods of earth. And how shall a staff dig out loose sand? Then, what was their use? The staff is a symbol of authority, as we see with the rods of Moses and Aaron. It was a question of the staff of office. It showed who was in authority and it was with these staves that they 'digged'.

Writes Paul to the young minister of the gospel, 'Let no man despise thee': thy calling and authority from God, let no man despise this. The nobles digged, not the people, but they digged for the common people and they loved the people for whom they digged. They digged with staves which by any standard—and on any ground—is a peculiar tool with which to dig. So then, what is the meaning?

You will remember that the Philistines used to fill in the wells of Abraham with rubbish. So intent were they upon this malicious work that constantly Isaac was forced to dig out the wells of his father in order to water the flocks. But so vile were the Philistines that no sooner had Isaac departed again, than these enemies once more filled in the wells and promptly added the insult of renaming them with other names.

Now, generations later, when the children of Israel came again into the land of their fathers' pilgrimage, they knew from the divine records that the ancient wells were hereabout in this country. Moreover, in every sense they had travelled the pilgrim way of Abraham. Why, they had got as far as Abraham their father, who was justified by faith, they were on the same ground.

They knew the well was here somewhere, but where exactly? As refilled of old, the ground would be monotonously level. But it was only a question of locating the general area; for then they could probe the earth for comparative softness. Spades were not needed, you see: staves, probes, would indicate just where on the level ground the soft area of the refilled shaft was situated: for in such a climate, preservation was phenomenal.

The shaft had been dug before and the ground must needs be softer; and when they probed with their staves still further, it was softer yet. So it was 'digging' with staves; 'searching' for what was once 'prepared'. Others had laboured, you see, and they were entering into their labours.

Even though generations had passed; despite that the Philistines had filled in every reminder of Abraham with earth and rubbish; notwithstanding all, princes and nobles shall soon rediscover the wells of Abraham, Isaac, and Jacob. They shall straightway find where the earth gives way, because the well shaft had been filled with soft matter as compared with the barren rocks and baked earth that had never been excavated from time immemorial.

They were nobles but humbly they still had to 'dig' with staves and the wells had to be dug to direction. They were shut up by direction to dig there. They were shut up to search and probe in this place of holy revelation. There was a director over them, and staves were the tools he required.

Now others have found the apostolic wells before us; they have taken the ground of the holy scriptures, and with a witness probed by direction, and they have found water. They have cleared the wells of the rubbish of false interpretation, do you see? And now it is our turn. For I can tell you there is still plenty to dig up.

It must be one's desire to be found a true Isaac—a well-opener—opening the wells of our father Abraham which the Philistines of church history have filled up. To be found a true child of Abraham; to prove the life that is beyond death; to see by faith things not seen by sight; to uncover *all* the wells and right to the bottom too, down to the living waters; this is what marks out the 'chosen seed of Ab'ram's race'.

Such digging is a labour of love and a work of faith and it is arduous, requiring patience of hope and a real work of grace—a work is uncovered, do you see? But as one meditates upon what Christ has done and who he is, one cannot help but sing praises. For the well flows and it springs up, but first it requires 'digging'. It is our turn now. Let us 'dig'—search; prepare—for ourselves.

5. The Director

The text reads, 'By the direction of the Lawgiver'. It is perfectly true that the words 'the direction of' are not in the original; they are an interpolation. The Hebrew simply reads 'By the Lawgiver'. Now whilst I disapprove most strongly of translators interpolating words and inserting their explanations into the page of holy scripture, I do not deny that 'By the direction of' agrees with the drift and force of the passage.

More to the point is the question, Who is the Lawgiver? Of course, many would say, Moses. After all, he was actually present on this occasion, and was the one that led the people. Still others would support this, saying, 'the law was given by Moses' *ergo* he is the Lawgiver.

Some will add, when 'law' is referred to in the old testament, almost invariably it is the Mosaic law that is the subject. Two hundred and seventeen times the word *Torah* occurs, and out of this number two hundred and sixteen times this has been translated 'Law', meaning the law of God given by Moses.

We will be told that the translation 'Lawgiver' in Numbers 21:18 must point to Moses. Law is associated with Moses. Thus it is supposed that the 'Law' actually 'given' refers to the *Torah*, the word used overwhelmingly for the Mosaic law. From this follows the unwarranted assumption that it has been proved that the 'Lawgiver' was Moses. But my brethren, surely we have learned to prod the surface a little more than that, yes?

For one thing, although *Torah* — the law of Moses — occurs two hundred and seventeen times, it is not the word for 'Law' in our text. And if not, then the passage is not likely to refer to the Mosaic lawgiver, either. Indeed, does this word in Numbers 21:18 really mean 'Lawgiver' at all? Not really. Certainly not primarily. The word is *Chaqaq* and it means 'cut', 'carve', 'engrave', 'picture'. The root idea is properly 'to cut', 'cut into', 'hack'.

Someone may object, But Moses cut or engraved the commandments upon the tables of stone. Moses? Oh? 'And the tables were the work *of God*, and the writing was the writing *of God*, graven upon the tables', Exodus 32:16. And indeed, that is a unique word for 'graven': not *chaqaq* but *charath.*

But my questioner may pursue me and say, Moses engraved the law—and was therefore the Lawgiver—the second time. No. The second time it was 'Hew *thee* two tables of stone like unto the first: and *I* will write upon these tables.' So Jehovah gave the *Torah*, but it came by Moses.

Besides, consider what was being directed by the 'Lawgiver'. The obtaining of water from the well. Numbers 21:16, 'I will give them water.' But this is a figure of the Holy Ghost, 'The water that I shall give'. But who said that? Moses? Not Moses. John 4:14 tells me it was Jesus: 'But whosoever drinketh of the water that I shall give him shall never thirst; but the water that I shall give him shall be in him a well of water springing up into everlasting life.'

But a moment's reflection will show that this expression cannot possibly refer to Moses. What saith the scripture? 'While Peter yet spake these words, the Holy Ghost fell on all them which heard the word.' Not whilst Peter was reading the direction of the law of Moses, notice, for he had long done that and been dry as dust. But while he preached the word of the gospel of Christ: then the Spirit fell; then the promise came; then the well was opened. Not to them which worked the law, mark, but on them which 'heard the word'.

'Received ye the Spirit by the works of the law, or by the hearing of faith?' The law truly came by Moses, but the Spirit did not. Grace and truth came by Jesus Christ, and so did the Holy Ghost. Jesus himself declares as concerning the Spirit: 'I will send him unto you'; not Moses will. John the Baptist, who represented the law, clearly identified the one who should open the wells of God. It is 'he which baptizeth with the Holy Ghost.' 'And I saw, and bare record that this is the Son of God.'

To the woman at the well Jesus said, 'If thou knewest the gift of God, and who it is that saith to thee, Give me to drink; thou wouldest have asked of him, and he would have given thee living water.' He would have given it, because he is the Director, the 'Lawgiver'. For, doubtless, 'This spake he of the Spirit, which they that believe on him should receive.'

Why then the ambiguous word 'Lawgiver' in Numbers 21:18? Is that the best rendering in English for the Hebrew word? I think it is far from the best rendering. Moreover I consider—bearing in mind the numerical supremacy of *Torah*, law, and the inevitable association of Moses with the law—that to render a totally different and much less used word 'Lawgiver' is both confusing and misleading. Especially when the reference is to Messias and not Moses.

However, let the reader judge. Consider the evidence: the word *chaqaq* occurs only nineteen times in scripture. It is either in verb or noun form. Used as a verb nine times, it has been translated variously: 'To appoint, decree, grave'; 'to note, pourtray, set'; 'to be printed'. Of the other ten references all are in noun form. As a noun the translators have given us: Governor, Decree, Lawgiver—six references—and Law. The grammatical forms vary more than I have shown, but this, broadly, is the picture.

We are to bear in mind that the basic conception of the word *chaqaq* is 'To cut', 'cut into', 'carve', 'engrave'. Whilst this may be applied to one who engraves or inscribes his decrees—admittedly as does a lawgiver—the *raison d'être* is not because he is a lawgiver, but because incidentally a lawgiver may inscribe or engrave. But in any event so do many other persons, officials, and functionaries.

Such as a scribe: '*Note* it in a book', Isaiah 30:8. Or one who models in clay: 'Thou also, son of man, take thee a tile ... and *pourtray* upon it the city', Ezekiel 4:1. Also a quarryman:

'Heweth him out a sepulchre ... and that *graveth* an habitation for himself in a rock', Isaiah 22:16. A painter also: 'Images *pourtrayed* with vermilion', Ezekiel 23:14. Even the Creator, Proverbs 8:29, 'He *appointed* the foundations of the earth.' It can mean governor, Judges 5:9, 'My heart is toward the *governors* of Israel.' All these—alike translated from *chaqaq*—engrave, cut, decree, every bit as much as any so-called 'Lawgiver'.

Therefore it follows that this view of Numbers 21:18 is an assumption on the part of the translators. Far more legitimate would be 'Governor' or 'Engraver'. The Septuagint in fact gives a totally different rendering with the idea of 'Lordship'. I suppose the translators thought it was Moses, implied that opinion with 'Lawgiver', and added the interpolation 'by the direction of' for good measure.

Why not 'Gracegiver'? It is just as good a translation; and it has the advantage of being accurate. If one objects that this does not answer to the context of Numbers 21:18, I reply, Does it not? 'I will *give* them water'? If it be pressed, But there is nothing graven, *chaqaq*, about the giving of grace, I reply: 'I have graven, *chaqaq*, thee upon the *palms of my hands*', Isaiah 49:16.

Why! except some actually put their finger into the print of the nails they will not believe the Gracegiver. But he giveth more grace, saying, 'Reach hither thy finger, and behold my hands.'

The few other '*Chaqaq*' texts in which the translators have imposed the rendering 'Lawgiver' confirm that it is Christ to whom the Hebrew refers, and not Moses. For example, Genesis 49:10, 'The sceptre shall not depart from Judah, nor a 'lawgiver' from between his feet, until Shiloh come; and unto him shall the gathering of the people be.' It is said expressly that the 'Lawgiver'—*chaqaq*—is from the tribe of Judah. But Moses is not from the tribe of Judah, rather, he is of Levi; and by that tribe came the law, not the '*Chaqaq*'.

But grace and truth came by Jesus Christ the son of David who was the son of Judah. And he is the long-awaited 'Grace-giver'. So confirms the writer of the epistle to the Hebrews: 'For it is evident that our Lord sprang out of Juda', Hebrews 7:14.

Under the title '*Chaqaq*' ancient Jacob spoke of Christ as springing from Judah: and moreover he did so—in Genesis 49:10—over four hundred years *before* the word was used again in Numbers 21:18. Now tell me, can anyone seriously suppose that this same title could then apply to Moses?

So then, ages before the incident in Numbers 'at the direction of the Lawgiver', Christ was prophesied of as coming from *Judah* in the name of 'Lawgiver'. And to crown all this, the selfsame prophecy — Genesis 49:10 — states: 'Unto him shall the *gathering* of the people be.' Four centuries later the incident in Numbers 21:16-18 commences with the words of Jehovah: '*Gather* the people together, and I will give them water.'

'Judah is my Lawgiver'—or rather, *Chaqaq*—confirms Jehovah centuries further on again, and for a witness repeats the statement, Psalms 60:7 and 108:8. And, cries the prophet Isaiah, 'The LORD is our Lawgiver', Isaiah 33:22. Now, in no way at all can any of these passages refer to Moses, to whom the legal covenant is indeed exclusive. For one thing—as to the two passages in the Psalms—Moses is of Levi not Judah; whereas the 'Lawgiver' is twice declared to be of Judah and not Levi. And for another thing—regarding Isaiah—Moses had no deity, that being the divine prerogative of the Son of David.

For it is evident, the so-translated 'Lawgiver'—Governor, or even Gracegiver: in any event, the '*Chaqaq*'—of Numbers 21:18 is both of Judah as to his humanity, and also of the Godhead as to his deity. This refers to the unique person of Christ. It is Christ Jesus upon whose hands—feet and side—the salvation of his people has been graven, and graven by grace alone springing of nothing but love divine.

As the Engraver the Lord inscribes the law of the Spirit of life in Christ Jesus upon our minds, and writes the same in our hearts. Thus we are manifestly the epistle of Christ written not with ink, nor graven with tool of man's device, but with the Spirit of the living God. Not in tables of Stone, mind, but in fleshy tables of the Heart. Cries the *Chaqaq* from the glory: 'I will put my laws into their hearts, and in their minds will I write them; and their sins and iniquities will I remember no more.'

Now blessed be God and the Father for the Governor, the Director, the Gracegiver who leads us into all truth, giving us this ministry whereby we may be enabled to open unto you these very wells of salvation by Christ Jesus. Blessed be God, I say; and as the Lord opens the flowing fountain to you at his direction, do you shout for joyfulness and cry aloud in singing at this blissful gift of grace: 'Spring up, O well; sing ye unto it.'

And now surely ye shall draw water—the water, saith your Lord, that I shall give you—with joy from the wells of salvation.

O sing unto the Lord; for he hath done excellent things: this is known in all the earth.

Cry out and shout, thou inhabitant of Zion: for great is the Holy One of Israel in the midst of thee.

Even so. Amen and Amen.

THE SEVENTH ADDRESS

The Seventh Address

Therefore with joy shall ye draw water out of the wells of salvation.

Isaiah 12:3.

The New Testament Fulfilment of 'Drawing Water with Joy': The Epistle of Paul the Apostle to the Philippians

TO conclude this exposition of Isaiah 12:3, I want to consider its joyful fulfilment. Clearly this is a passage which is prophetic of the new testament, referring as it does to the ministration of the Spirit. Then it must be after Calvary, beyond Golgotha, and consequent upon Pentecost that we are to look for its true realization.

Certainly it is true that the water which Christ gives is drawn by us with joy; but not until it was obtained by him with anguish. This is pictured for us by the flow from the riven side of the stricken and slain Saviour upon the tree: 'And forthwith came there out blood and water.'

To see this in another figure. It was after the Rock was smitten that the waters gushed forth; *then* 'they drank of that spiritual Rock that followed them: and that Rock was Christ', I Cor. 10:4.

Let me remind you that the wells of salvation are first and foremost divine wells. They are the deeps of the experimental knowledge of God as Saviour. Therefore the first definite, precise observation regarding the wells of salvation is that they represent the revealed knowledge of God.

This involves three things, as you have been taught. It involves the knowledge of the Father. It involves the knowledge of the Son. It involves the knowledge of the Holy Ghost. The wells of salvation stand in the revelation of three divine Persons in one Godhead, and this knowledge is life eternal: 'That they might know thee the only true God, and Jesus Christ, whom thou hast sent.'

Then secondly, the wells of salvation are doctrinal wells: they stand in the knowledge of the gospel. They set forth what God has done to save his people, and they do so by the revelation of the truth in the new testament of our Lord and Saviour Jesus Christ. The wells represent the great doctrines of the evangel, the faith once delivered to the saints.

The gospel wonderfully opens up the precious truth revealed by the death and in the broken body and shed blood of the Lord Jesus at the cross. The doctrine then views the resurrection and ascension of the Son, and in consequence teaches the sanctifying work of the Holy Ghost. Finally the tremendous truths ushered in at the return of the Lord from heaven are richly clustered and embodied in the faith of the evangel. These are the things which are signified by the gospel wells of salvation.

But if these wells are to bring saving grace to our souls, we ourselves must actually drink from the waters. In other words the knowledge must not only be revealed but also be communicated. One must be personally refreshed. That was why, on previous occasions, we considered how water is to be drawn from the wells of salvation.

You will remember that although Isaiah 12:3 refers to the gospel day nevertheless it was wonderfully prefigured in the book of Numbers. The children of Israel, being gathered together, sang to the well. It is true that the nobles digged with their staves, yet notwithstanding it was the singing of Israel that raised the water.

But now I want to expound the way in which these joyful issues are described not in type but in reality. That is, not in a figure of the fulfilment of the text but in the actual fulfilment of the text. Not from the old testament enactment but from the new testament verification. Let us see from a personal situation in the new testament where the age-old prophecy is being substantiated and realized in actuality.

The selection of a new testament example of one drawing water with joy from the wells of salvation is not difficult. Instances abound, but one excelleth them all. Because joy and freshness always follow the flowing of the water of life—and since this is drawn solely from the wells of salvation—where these qualities are most conspicuous there will be found the foremost illustration.

The choice example positively radiates with joyfulness. It diffuses a fragrance of Christ that lingers on the very atmosphere. Yet it is derived not from an environment of tranquil retreat within some idyllic setting, but in circumstances of trial, imprisonment, chains, and bonds.

Of course, I refer to the apostle Paul in the epistle to the saints at Philippi. In this short letter of four chapters we find the words joy or rejoice occurring no less than eighteen times. The word in one or other of its forms occurs five times in chapter 1, seven times in chapter 2, twice in chapter 3, and four times in the last chapter.

And that is but the word, the mention, of joy and rejoicing: let alone the fact of it. These instances, so prolific in the space of four small chapters, but serve to indicate the occasional surfacing of what is in fact the rich, deep, underlying strata.

1. The Background of Philippians

When one considers the background of tribulation to this epistle, it is obvious that no one could maintain joy in such circumstances were he not drawing upon divine resources.

Despite the most adverse and miserable environment to the contrary, the apostle Paul was not only unmoved but positively radiant. He was a prisoner of the State. Roman soldiers guarded him and kept him close captive day and night. He was chained. He was awaiting trial at Caesar's pleasure with a real possibility of condemnation. The sentence would follow: death by execution.

He could not preach. He was able to write and receive visitors but without question his heart was in preaching and for years past—years, mark it—at Jerusalem, Caesarea, in the journey to Rome and at Rome, he had neither preached nor had he visited the churches. Years of terrible burden had been his; he longed to preach in the regions beyond yet now could not preach in the street adjoining.

But a worse burden lay upon him; though it would not be burdensome to carnal men. The worst burden was the state of the church. False teachers were arising and many had been drawn after them. Subtle perversions of the gospel abounded, but all alike were flattering to man, appealing to works, and suited to self-righteousness.

At Rome these hireling shepherds preached freely, but with secret spite, hoping to add affliction to the faithful apostle who was in chains. Why? Because they hated Paul, together with his cross-exalting pride-debasing gospel. They could not stomach the grand doctrines of free grace. Whilst silence was enforced upon Paul, they openly published their legal 'other gospel'. They did what the apostle could not do because of his faithfulness: they preached.

It was legal Judaizers that had caused Paul's imprisonment. He was prevented by no chain other than faithfulness. He would not have had a chain had he but compromised the evangel with their legal mixture. My bonds in Christ, he says, The prisoner of the Lord. His chains would have dropped off if he had done what they did: he was a prisoner because he put fidelity before the mere love of preaching.

As the years of Paul's imprisonment lengthened so the church increased more and more with false brethren; many false brethren had crept in, at first unawares, then openly. Supported by the influence of uncalled and unspiritual teachers, these became established and waxed bolder and bolder.

The old divines, the old gospel, the old heavenly ways, the old sweet separation to Christ, the old meek spirituality of communion: these things were being put in jeopardy and were beginning to go out already. Already!

Many walked as enemies of the cross. Many made a fair show in the flesh. Many loved the praise of men more than the praise of God. The god of many was their belly, they minded earthly things. Pharisees at heart, scribes in the head, their affection for self-righteousness perverted the evangel and defiled the holy law of God into moralizing legality. Why? Because it gave them somewhat in which to preen themselves, something in which to boast, and in their secret heart of hearts they swelled with self-love, self-esteem, and self-justification.

To the heart-broken grief of the apostle, this in the churches was beginning to affect the church as a whole. There had come in — he tells us even weeping — this walking in the flesh, this carnal conversation, this minding of earthly things. There was a dangerous new grieving of the Spirit, and there was a new shunning of the old fearless preaching.

Novelties were taking the place of the everlasting gospel. The old preachers had brought down the dews of Canaan, the atmosphere of eternity, the breath from another world. The coming of Christ was a felt reality; the Holy City was thrillingly sensed; one veritably tingled at the imminence of the glory yet to be revealed. *Where had this gone?*

And what of the straightforward preaching on sin, righteousness, and judgment to come? What of the lawful use of the law? Where was the awful judgment preaching, the solemn weeping countenance of the preacher as he warns of the fiery deluge reserved for the wicked in the day of wrath: *where was this now?*

There was a new discomfort at the old evangel, a new departing from the holy fellowship, and new ceremonies for old ordinances. The self-seeking and lawless were stridently arising in the midst of the church, they were taking the parts of the gospel that suited them, and going out in a way of worldly ambition.

Already there was a great departure from that pure doctrine, from the Spirit-filled, God-indwelt, separated Body of Christ—the Bride. And this broke the apostle's heart beyond measure, and continually affected him even to tears.

2. The Occasion of Philippians

Such were the conditions in which, without warning, the Roman hallway echoed with Macedonian accents. Looking up to the entrance, Paul would have seen the totally unexpected arrival of Epaphroditus, laden as he was with messages and gifts from across the sea, from the saints at Philippi.

The Macedonian came with firm assurances from the brethren of a bold stand together with the apostle in the truth of the gospel. They were not tolerating hireling shepherds or receiving false brethren at Philippi. Let Paul rest assured. Epaphroditus conveyed to the apostle the strongest affirmation of striving in one spirit together with one mind for the faith of the gospel, no matter what happened in the world, no, nor in the church, and certainly not in the ministry.

But suddenly Epaphroditus fell sick. With an abruptness equal to that of his arrival he weakened and hovered on the brink of death. Paul had been so comforted by his arrival and now—sorrow upon sorrow—feared for the effects of the illness, not least upon the church at Philippi. However the sick man survived the crisis and was strengthened, soon to be restored to health again.

Finally Paul sends Epaphroditus—by whom at the first he had received such magnanimous bounty from the saints at Philippi —back to that city, fully recovered, carrying this very letter in his hand, a copy of which is now within your possession.

Although serious enough to the participants at the time, viewed against the context of history, the occasion of this epistle seems trivial. Really it is no more than a letter of thanks, sent by hand; what you would call a 'thank-you' letter. But when the donor is a spiritual church, holding to the truth of the gospel; and when the recipient is the holy apostle, suffering for the gospel's sake: then such a responsive letter kindled by inspiration soars from the commonplace to the priceless, so as by sheer worth to survive the millennia.

If so, then the most mundane matters may be used by the united if despised saints and by the faithful if suffering ministers of the word as an occasion to diffuse the fragrance of Christ and the issues of the Spirit.

Now observe, I am not drawing petty lessons. I am addressing myself to the correct application of the epistle. Its proper relevance is to the saints gathered by the Holy Ghost under powerful gospel preaching, and in connection with vital spiritual ministers holding a cruelly persecuted testimony. I am speaking of an isolated apostle and not only isolated but bitterly maligned. It is that fellowship and union between the apostle Paul in those conditions and the saints at Philippi in that situation which brought forth the spiritual savour of this epistle.

Only a true affinity with the correspondents can honestly warrant its genuine application. Except we find ourselves in parallel circumstances we cannot possibly see eye to eye in experience with either the writer or the recipients. Thus it is clear that this epistle is not a letter from some nobody to anybody to be applied as all and sundry think fit. It is the inspired communication from just such a minister of the gospel to exactly those saints called out of the world at Philippi there to be the assembly of God's people.

Then albeit that the occasion of the letter was relatively trivial, the letter itself is not. It is weighty, divine, and powerful in the extreme. It reveals the sweet fervour of gospel relationships. It shows the apostle's love for the brethren at Philippi, a love so tender and of such profound concern that when Paul prays he is either crying for joy or weeping with earnestness; so did he love the saints.

He is both touched and moved by their stand with him in the truth of the gospel when this was neither common nor easy. He is plainly full of intense gratitude for their confirming and defending of the faith and their fidelity to the ministry committed unto him.

They are in complete unity with him. They are absolutely, totally heart and soul with him, they love him and he loves them. These gospel relationships are far more intense than any family bond, they are far more inward, noble, and sublime than any human relationship or any love found among men, or between men and women.

The love of God kindles these bonds, eternity cradles them, the gospel nurtures them. Such relationships are intense and spiritual: they flow from love divine, all loves excelling. This is that profound and unique affection that stands between the minister of the gospel and those whom he has begotten in the Lord; he has cherished them: nursed, weaned, and established them in the faith: O, it is inexpressible. Unspeakable. Divine.

This epistle describes the lot that fell to Paul during his detainment, revealing a great deal about the apostle's personal situation and relationships. It shows how he met various trials, smiled at adversity, overcame every obstacle, was victorious in all his temptations, and kept himself in the love of God, rejoicing in Christ Jesus, and having no confidence in the flesh.

Notice also the apostle's total disregard for his own earthly, bodily, and worldly interests. Heart and mind are taken up, absorbed, with the Lord and with the saints. He exhorts the brethren fervently and you can see from the first stroke of his pen to the last, that he is not thinking of himself at all: he is thinking only of them as in the Lord, all the time. And not as though he were striving to do so, or trying to fulfil his duty: it is spontaneous, he can't help it, he loves them.

Though persecuted, death a real possibility, heart-broken over the state of the church, without bitterness or rancour his spirit is kept fresh and sweet.

He bids the saints observe Christ in Christ's utmost trial, meek unto death; this is eminent in the epistle. Wherefore, he says, God hath highly exalted him and given him a name which is above every name. That is what he is looking at—Oh, tongue cannot express—he is not looking at anything between him and death, he is not looking at death: he can't see it. His vision *starts* beyond death, he is enwrapt with Christ.

And consider, this was written amidst bonds and imprisonments, in an atmosphere of bleak depression, with the future dark and threatening. Rejoice in the Lord, says the apostle.

Count it all joy, my brethren, says another. Therein I do rejoice, yea, and will rejoice; this is the secret of the seven uncut locks of Paul's head. 'And again I say, Rejoice.'

3. Joy in Philippians

Now I purpose to show you the joy with which the apostle Paul obtained the water of life, and the wells from which he drew so abundantly. However before doing so I would again stress the importance of keeping in mind the arid wilderness with which Paul was surrounded.

When considering the joy that glows from the pages of Philippians, it is so very easy to forget that at the same time the apostle walked under the most appalling circumstances. Often he was heart-broken and in tears, not for himelf but for others; death itself loomed imminent. As to the state of the church and of the Lord's testimony, Paul was under the most immense mental burden and spiritual anguish.

Meanwhile he was suffering under the severe test of providence resulting from his inability to preach the gospel despite his call to do so. Enchained, he had the provocation, not to say mockery, of uncalled self-seekers freely preaching an admixture of law and gospel that might enchant but would certainly damn the hearers. O agony of Paul! Mark that, his inability to preach the gospel despite the desperate need that he should do so.

Now what a dreadful array of soul-torturing questions the tempter sets before the apostle. A 'Why?' to frustrate; an 'How?' to fret; a 'When?' to rack the heart. Cruel queries, the slings and arrows of outraged Satan, set with barbs and hooks to twist, gouge, lacerate, and fix fast within the soul. But valiant Paul brings up the shield of faith, wherewith he turns the lance, deflects the arrows, dashes the thrusts, and quenches all the fiery darts of the wicked. He will allow no miserable, unbelieving queries to so much as enter his ears. Such questions are so far beneath his contempt that he disdains even to admit, much less acknowledge, their existence.

No room is allowed for doubt or despair. On the contrary, by committing everything to prayer Paul experiences the peace of God which passes understanding. He is full of joy and rejoicing and he is determined to maintain it and remain so. He will not be cast down. He will not entertain so much as a whisper of doubt. He won't even consider unbelieving murmurs. He knows what to be joyful about: the Lord. The Lord!

Notice that when the apostle says, Rejoice in the Lord, he does not speak of the Saviour in the sole name of Jesus, or even of that name at all. There is a ring of authority about the title 'Lord'. It does not brook argument. It is autocratic. It requires total submission. Peremptorily it demands humble awe on the part of the subject: 'Lord!'

To speak of or pray concerning the untitled name of Jesus is both legitimate and spiritual *if* used in the proper context: that is, as indicating his person seen on earth in the gospels, during his humiliation. Legitimate, I say, if it be used in the proper context.

But make no mistake: that is *not* of the Spirit which would lead men indiscriminately to address the Lord Jesus upon what are to all intents and purposes 'Christian name' terms. It is contrary to scripture, and against all social decency. It would be upstart and impudent enough towards Her Majesty the Queen. But towards the King of kings it is utterly shocking. Such impertinence predicates towering and conceited ignorance. Those who actually see the Lord respond with one accord: 'My Lord and my God.' 'And when I saw him, I fell at his feet as dead.'

The epistles do not refer to the Son of God in the unqualified name of 'Jesus' unless pointing back to the Saviour as on earth in the meek and lowly context of his humiliation. Or unless stressing that it is he, the lowly One—'this *same* Jesus'—that is now so gloriously vindicated in the title of both 'Lord' and 'Christ'.

In other words, since the ascension and the formation of the church, the name 'Jesus' refers to him *as he was*, but the titles 'Lord' and 'Christ' speak of him *as he is*.

Therefore, note, in this place it does not say, Rejoice in Jesus: rather, it is Rejoice in the Lord. Consequently the title 'Lord' would indicate his being beyond and outside all the circumstances through which he once travailed and suffered on earth. It would show his having entered into the joy that hitherto had been set before him. It would indicate our rejoicing in him as risen and ascended.

Rejoicing in the 'Lord' involves the saints in an interior awareness of participation in Christ as now risen and ascended and thus beyond the reach of fleshly conditions, earthly states, and worldly circumstances. Paul may be in them but the Lord is over them. The Lord Jesus is not in them, he died out of them and Paul is saying, I, whilst in them, Rejoice in the 'Lord'.

The unchanging truth of the gospel, the unalterable doctrine of salvation, the faith once delivered to the saints: these were like immovable rock to Paul. He loved the truth. He was mentally keyed into that rock. He was emotionally anchored to it, so that when the rain descended, and the floods came, and the winds blew, and beat upon him: he fell not; for he was founded upon a rock.

I am not saying he was not blown, but he was not blown away, he was not tossed to and fro and carried about with every wind of doctrine.

He knew exactly what to believe about the great doctrinal truths of the faith. He had learned the truth, the whole truth, and nothing but the truth about justification, sanctification, and redemption. He had a mind stayed on divine Persons and things: upon Father, Son, and Holy Ghost. Upon the word of salvation. Upon the things that Father, Son, and Holy Ghost have done in salvation. Thus was Paul sustained and daily refreshed from the wells of salvation.

Living by faith, rejoicing in the Lord, Paul's mind was stayed on things holy and heavenly; things unaffected by history, oblivious to news, unaltered by tumults, undefiled by learning, unspoilt by reasoning, unembittered by poverty, unadulterated by riches, contemptuous of fashions, superior to the whole world, and elevated over time itself.

Mark too that the source of his joy and thinking was in the Spirit; this is incomparably deeper than the flesh and it is infinitely more profound than squalid reasonings, carnal musings, legal strivings, natural sensations, and withal than emotional outbursts about a 'Jesus' known after the flesh.

Not only were Paul's roots out of this world and into Christ, but all his springs were in him. And, as we have seen, his foundations also were outside this present realm, keyed into the gospel. Surely, his soul was beyond the reach of all things adverse: whether things past, present, or to come. Not only his roots, springs, and foundations, but moreover his inmost union was with and in Christ alike rooted and grounded in love.

Not simply in the letter. Paul's confidence did not stand in mental assent to a few gospel texts about a merely descriptive way of salvation. His assurance was not in what was letter-ish, neither in fleshly feelings, nor in variable transience. No more was it in natural or rational thought with its concomitant deadly unbelief. But alike roots, springs, foundations, union with Christ, and the witness of assurance were secured in the living God.

It was God that had laid hold on Paul: When it pleased God, he said, to reveal his Son in me. When it pleased God to call me by his grace. I say again, roots, springs, foundations, union, witness, and all things past, present, and future; things in this world and things in that which is to come: all to Paul were alike safe with God, and in God, and of God, and from God. Say, is it any wonder he rejoiced?

The gospel of God concerning his Son was that which the apostle loved and elevated clear of every pollution from human philosophy, or mixture from the old legal system. No one else possessed such clarity. Paul had discarded with disgust and horror anything he might achieve of himself in religion: I count it as dung. Dung! With disgust and horror. Anything at all that might be rooted in nature, fused by law, wrought by works, or graven with art or man's device.

He would not even claim those promises in the scripture to which he did not feel a savoury union and unction in the Spirit. To him, coldly of themselves they were the dead letter that killed: it was the Spirit who took them and ministered life by faith through them to his soul.

No, the apostle had been laid hold upon by God and that with might by his Spirit in the inner man. This was the way in which he began and by this same rule he would continue and endure to the end.

The overwhelming love of God had arrested, then filled the apostle Paul within the hidden man of the heart. Beyond the realm of the flesh, love divine dwelt in that interior which was heaven-born and God-begotten. This was the new man, the inner man, and therein Paul was strengthened with might by God's Spirit. This new man was stronger than the old; though the old lusted against it and fought continually for supremacy.

But Paul kept one thing clearly and unconfusedly in view: *God* had laid hold on him. In times of utmost trial and tribulation, under ominous clouds of darkness, he held onto this: it was *God* that had called him. As thus chosen, laid hold upon, born within, divinely secured, and as knowing a present union in the Holy Ghost, he could never doubt what God had done, was doing, and would yet do for him in Christ.

The joy of the apostle was in the Lord and his heart and mind were enlarged and meditative in the gospel: contemplative in God. His whole mentality was stayed. He was not, when he felt the sweet sensation, drawing water out of the wells of joy. But with joy, though he felt anguish within and knew fears without, he was drawing water out of the wells of salvation.

Day and night in psalms and hymns and spiritual songs, in heavenly melody and in sweet psalmody, though his voice was breaking, his heart was fixed. No matter what his outward afflictions or his inward sufferings, with a more profound interior joy from superior, divine, objective truth Paul drew water out of the wells of salvation and rhapsodized in his heart to the Lord. At midnight he sung praises unto the LORD.

The apostle is seen as completely devoted, moved by selfless, pure, and divine love. He only mentions himself at all when it is obviously to the distinct benefit of the brethren. Yet to learn one's heart with even the most elementary degree of self-knowledge reveals nothing but a rock-like core, a stony heart of unbelief, full of unmitigated adamant self-interest; it is total selfishness. Then see in Paul how regeneration breaketh the rock in pieces, rends the core asunder, takes it all away, and freely by grace gives a new heart, a spiritual, kindly, and tender heart of flesh.

The apostle's unworldliness is equally conspicuous. Even so far as the ultimate question of death itself, well, for him to leave the body: that is not death. If he looked at it with worldly and carnal eyes it might be so considered, but he does not look at it in that way. He does not consider it as death, to him it is not death. To die is gain.

He is occupied with everlasting life, with a better resurrection, with a body 'like unto his glorious body'. He is quite freely and happily resigned as to leaving the body. Far from death, it is life. He welcomes it. And this welcoming is utterly genuine, there is no cant or humbug about it. The only reason he prefers to stay on in this world is in order to do good to the saints at his own personal cost. Today, 'theologians' talk of 'comparative religions'. What comparison? And church leaders regale us with 'other faiths'. What faith? There is *nothing but* the gospel that abolishes both death and the fear of it, and brings life and immortality to light; it is *the* faith. Just as there is none other name given under heaven among men whereby we must be saved.

As to property, if Paul had any, he doesn't mention it. He is careless of it, either way—whether more or less. He has had more and he has had less but he rejoices in the Lord and he is indifferent to this world's goods. He has known great abundance and he has had bitter poverty. Abased or abounding, he is quite indifferent.

Regarding the gift from Philippi, the very occasion of the letter, this does not find a place until the end. When he does come to thanking them for it, he is completely taken up with what is spiritual in the giving, not with the gift itself.

All that really matters to the apostle in such a gift is the treasure of love in the heart of the givers. He is full of the spiritual significance of this generous giving. Paul is occupied completely with allusions to the wonderful gifts of God that transformed the hearts of men into such a shining reflection of divine generosity.

A major lesson to be learnt from this epistle as regards the saints' joy is that the church—whatever the circumstances—ought always to stand uncompromisingly for the gospel. To obtain the joy of the Lord, the saints must necessarily reject every error, every worldly intrusion, and side openly and stand publicly with the despised, ostracized, and even imprisoned faithful ministers of the gospel.

This is exactly what the church at Philippi did and this is the thing that made the apostle Paul so joyful. This is Paul's joy. He alludes to their faithful leaders in a unique tribute by writing to the 'bishops and deacons': the only epistle in which this occurs.

Worldly religion cannot tolerate what is spiritual, and of course the uncompromising loyalty of the church to the apostle's fidelity therefore brought religious ignominy and legal persecution to the saints.

They must needs go outside the camp, bearing Christ's reproach and tasting of the offence of the cross. Nevertheless, they could and did endure a great fight of afflictions. Certainly those early saints knew that they had in heaven a better and an enduring substance. Then what of today? We too must learn to look out of this world unto that which is to come, out of time into eternity, out of earthly circumstances up to the Lord, out of this body towards the body of the resurrection.

Moreover, in such a position the saints are to rejoice and to joy in the Lord, and again rejoice! They are to walk so as they have the apostle for an example: 'be ye followers of me, even as I am also of Christ.' They are to rise superior over the withering contempt of those who scorn both the apostle and his ministry. They are to be elevated over the sly jibes of the worldling against the heavenliness of such spiritual conversation. They are not to be afraid to suffer persecution with the true gospel minister as a church and as saints.

Indeed it is imperative for the brethren that they abide under the ministry; 'Take heed unto thyself', says the apostle to his successor in the work, 'and unto the doctrine; continue in them: for in doing this thou shalt both save thyself, and them that hear thee.'

If so, then how vital it must be for the brethren that Christ should continue to send such a ministry. How can we come to the truth without it? 'How shall they hear without a preacher? And how shall they preach, except they be sent?' And again 'He gave some, apostles; and some, prophets; and some, evangelists; and some, pastors and teachers; for the perfecting of the saints, for the work of the ministry, for the edifying of the body of Christ.' Now, when the saints have no necessity for perfecting; when the ministry no longer requires working; when the body of Christ has ceased to need edifying, then, then the ministry may be dispensed with as superfluous.

On the other hand the example of the great apostle to the preachers of the truth clearly shows us that the doctrine held and sounded out must first and foremost be lived in if one is to be a proper minister of the gospel. Faithfulness to what one says is far more important than saying it. And it may well come to pass, that by being true to what one preaches, one is thereby prevented from preaching.

But even if it should mean poverty, ostracism, imprisonment, or at the last death, it will be found that the suffering entailed —though once dreaded—becomes the very means by which is released the joy of heaven and which shall prove to be marrow and fatness to the bones of the saints. In itself, the breaking of the alabaster box of earthly care becomes that which diffuses abroad the sweet fragrance of Christ, and all that are in the house shall have it in memorial.

Fidelity to Christ is incomparably greater than preaching; and, put in the balance of choice, to trade fidelity for the right to preach is nothing more nor less than to love supremely the sound of one's own voice. In Paul's case, such fidelity and integrity resulted in the most pathetic circumstances. But was he faithless to Christ? Was he? Even in the smallest point of gospel integrity did he compromise so that he might continue preaching? Did he? Does one detect him reasoning, My preaching is more than mere details, and if such trifling things stop me preaching, it is better to 'lovingly yield' and be 'charitably silent' about what many 'respected brethren' consider 'relatively unimportant' points? Never. Never.

You see then that Paul was a saint primarily and a minister thereafter. 'He counted me faithful' firstly, 'putting me into the ministry' secondly. He was true to the Lord and the gospel in all his associations and in every condition.

As a minister he paid the ultimate price, because his fidelity cost him his ministry. Not only was he often misunderstood: so high did he ascend above the generality; but he was deliberately maligned and slandered with diabolical malice. This lost him many churches, alas! many of his own. It shut his mouth perforce, so far as preaching was concerned.

But did Paul therefore doubt the validity of his course? Never! He never doubted. Indeed, his consequent suffering and imprisonment became the very thing that set free and liberated such joy. It brought the overwhelming sympathy, the most intense love, the tenderest union from those who were spiritual: Paul's faithfulness was their rejoicing. And I would add, his very tribulation brought forth this letter from prison to be preserved across two thousand years of already immeasurable fruitfulness, now to be opened before your own eyes.

So then, the apostle Paul remained steadfast. This was despite the discouragement of many who could and did preach and who could and did mock Paul for his faithfulness to Christ and his gospel. Yet did they preach as Paul had, they would have come to where he was.

It is plain to see in this epistle both the inward and outward tribulations caused by the righteous testimony of the faithful gospel minister. The epistle encourages those who are in similar affliction and shows them that a spiritual walk may be maintained with profit, and joy also may be diffused by such despised followers of Christ. And this despite all the decline and apostasy in the church, and notwithstanding all the compromise and falling away throughout the ministry. Do you think that too sweeping? Consider Philippians 2:20,21; 'For I have no man likeminded, who will naturally care for your state. For all seek their own, not the things which are Jesus Christ's.'

Despite imposed silence, the apostle would not yield to bitterness or despair, much less to unbelief. He found a way to be useful notwithstanding, even if only by conversation and by correspondence. Instead of miserably railing at circumstances, he finds that wherein to rejoice. And remain profitable.

He maintains his diminished ministry by prayers, intercessions, and thanksgivings; by uttering or writing such few words and whispers as he is enabled right up to the very last. And—witness this fruitful epistle—in so doing, like Samson, he slew more in his death than in the whole of his life.

This epistle therefore reveals to us not so much what the apostle preached, but rather how he lived and died by what he preached. His was not a ministry of religious platitudes, his was a ministry of living sacrifice offered up in fidelity, withal finding strength for it as drawing water with joy from the wells of salvation.

One of the most vital lessons that the saints ought always to keep in mind is seen from the background of the epistle, where brethren and churches 'with one consent began to make excuse'. O, this propensity to go with the majority. '*All* we *like sheep* have gone astray.' But not the saints at Philippi. Alone or not, they neither knew, nor cared. *Christ, his gospel, and his ministry were enough for them.* Therefore we observe that a church—like the minister—may be kept faithful despite the unfaithfulness of other churches all around. 'This thou knowest, that all they which are in Asia be turned away from me', II Timothy 1:15. Yes, even churches raised up under Paul's own apostleship.

So then, a church may and ought to be true to the gospel and to the gospel's true ministers and loyal to them, despite what other churches or even the whole church may say or require.

Fidelity is not dependent upon others, whether other ministers, churches, or the whole professing church. When individuals start looking sideways and not upwards, danger has already struck. 'Look up, lift up your heads', saith Christ, 'for your redemption draweth nigh.' The weak propensity to follow the crowd had smitten the churches in the apostle's day, and it has blighted the church more and more ever since. This sheep-like attitude does not commence with actual evil: it commences with that *sapping of individuality* in which it is supposed that all good must be done as organized *en masse*. Once that pernicious error softens the backbone, evil becomes almost irresistible, provided only that pressure is gently applied, and above all is applied collectively.

Such weakness is an abomination. The organization and systematization of brethren and churches into sects, parties, denominations, federations, groups, amalgams, councils, unions, alliances: all this is the invented recourse of the unbelieving, the unspiritual, the unscriptural, and of the insecure. Christ is enough, yes, and more than enough: he was for Paul, and furthermore he was for the church at Philippi.

When this is genuinely so, how rich is the pure and intense love and the spiritual relations and affections between the faithful. This the epistle shows: how one can walk as a true minister and as a faithful church even up to this last day.

For we *should* walk unaffected by this world and what is in the world, being kept in that union which is in the Lord and with that congregation which dwells in the Father and the Son. This epistle teaches clearly how we can be kept faithful and rejoicing irrespective of all the accrued and current corruption, both in the world and in the professing church.

The saints will then have regard to the wells of salvation and the drawing of water with joy therefrom. Nothing less than these ideals of the new testament which are set before us in the word of God will face us in the day of judgment, and nothing less should be before our eyes during this short uncertain period of our pilgrimage.

Our relations therefore with the Lord and his gospel, with the Spirit and with God the Father, our relations with ministers of the gospel and the true churches, all these need not be affected. They need not be affected even to this day. Neither need our joy.

It is a question, as with the apostle Paul in this epistle, of dwelling and walking in what is unaffected by man and by the world and by time. Christ and his gospel, in the work of God, must be openly shown forth, cherished, maintained, and defended in the same way now as then; at all and every cost even unto the death. And I may add, whosoever endureth to the end, the same shall be saved.

4. The Source of Joy in Philippians

Now, finally, I wish to point briefly to those wells from which the apostle Paul drew so abundantly and to which he alludes so constantly in the Philippian epistle.

The epistle is not written to describe those wells of salvation, remark, but, even as Paul lived, moved, and had his being in the Spirit, so of necessity the writing of this letter found its spring in his soul from the living waters of the Holy Ghost. Then it is inevitable that both the well from which the water is drawn and the water drawn from it, appear constantly upon the written page.

From the beginning I have stressed that the wells of salvation are twofold in character. First, they represent the hidden depths of the knowledge of God as Saviour. Secondly, the wells indicate penetrating deeps into the knowledge of the truth of salvation. It is marvellous to observe in Paul's letter how abundantly the knowledge of the God of his salvation gave forth to the apostle the flowing waters of gospel experience, joyfully refreshing him throughout all his pilgrimage.

He is not speaking of that knowledge, remember, he is thanking the saints at Philippi and acquainting them with his state, but the spring and source of his heavenly support cannot be hidden. It appears on every page. Eighty times the names of God the Father, Son, and Holy Ghost occur in this epistle of four chapters, and in every occurrence one can see that the apostle's knowledge is that of immediate spiritual union and of vital conscious realization.

None but one full of Christ could speak so often of the Saviour in such a way. As his heart is inditing a good matter, his tongue is the pen of a ready writer, and so Paul speaks of the things he has made touching the King.

No less than fifty-five times reference is made to the Lord himself, and that under a total of no fewer than eleven personal names. If this is not the knowledge of God our Saviour in the Person of the Son, then, pray, what is?

And let us remind ourselves constantly that the epistle is not written to convey that knowledge, but is a simple letter of ordinary correspondence from the apostle to thank the saints for their provision. O, such holiness! When, O when, my soul, shall we attain it? But in thanking them, these living streams gush forth: see then the source of all genuine thanksgiving. If this is not with joy drawing water from the wells of salvation, what is?

Observe what hidden depths the apostle sounded in the knowledge of Christ Jesus our Lord. Eight times over he refers to him as Jesus Christ; nine times as Christ Jesus. Why the difference? Because the Lord is so profound, his sonship so marvellous, his being so stupendous, that nothing but such names conveyed by the Spirit reveal what was true of the Son in the actual reality of his wonderful Person.

Three times Paul speaks of the Saviour as the Lord Jesus Christ, and eighteen times as Christ. Eleven times as Lord, once as Jesus. He speaks of him as God, Man, Servant, Lord Jesus, and Saviour.

All these different views of his Person were so expressed because Paul really knew the Son of God, and by revelation saw him, just as by inward union he knew what it was to dwell in Christ and Christ in him. Then what wells of salvation there are in the knowledge of God our Saviour through the revelation of the Son. These cannot but appear in the epistle, because they are the source of Paul's joy.

One might ask oneself, how much was the Son of God mentioned in one's own last letter, though it were but a letter of thanks? Under what titles was Christ intelligently and feelingly perceived and uttered?

Four times the Holy Ghost is mentioned, though of these once he is called the 'Spirit of Jesus Christ'. Then what a perfect balance is seen in the relatively scarce references to that divine Person who does not speak of himself, but in lowly condescension comes to speak of Christ and glorify the Son of God.

How this shows up the various errors stressing gift or experience directly from the Spirit, each of which gives itself away by its constant over-emphasis of the Person of the Holy Ghost: and all so unbalanced as compared with scriptural proportions.

When divine Persons are truly revealed, their distinctive work is then clearly perceived, and it follows naturally that sound doctrine is inevitable in consequence. Any other sequence, system, teaching, or learning is utterly disastrous as regards divinity.

The great wells of salvation in God and the Father are alluded to some twenty-one times in the epistle. How the apostle rejoiced with trembling in the very presence of the God of his salvation. Fifteen times he speaks distinctly of God as such. He refers to God our Father, God the Father, God and our Father, the God of Peace, and with a fine personal turn speaks to them of 'my God'.

From all the foregoing references to Father, Son, and Holy Ghost, it is evident, more than evident, it is proof abundant, that the first great character of the wells of salvation is that of the knowledge of God himself. This is that from which Paul drew not only strength, but real joy: rejoice, he says, rejoice in 'the Lord'.

The preceding may suffice us as the clearest of examples showing the apostle with joy drawing water out of the wells of salvation. And if so, then from wells respecting the hidden depths of the revelation of God made known in three Persons through the knowledge of our Lord and Saviour Jesus Christ.

But what of the wells in the character of those penetrating deeps into the knowledge of what God has done in salvation: the truth of salvation itself; does Paul speak of this?

Yes, he does, and much every way. We read of working out our own salvation with fear and trembling, because it is God that worketh in us to will and to do of his good pleasure. As regards the gospel of our salvation, straightway we hear of the fellowship of the gospel, the defence of the gospel, and the confirmation of the gospel. Following this we have the furtherance of the gospel. Then we read of the gospel of Christ held in the faith of the gospel. The death of the cross is central, and the word of God essential.

What doctrinal wells now break forth upon our wondering eyes. Here is the deity of Christ, there the humanity of Christ, and withal the Person of Christ. Follows the sure work. Appears now his death, resurrection, ascension, and exaltation. Soon will be manifest the coming day of Christ.

For time and eternity endures majestic the peerless well of Justification by faith without the works of the law. But everything must be seen in connection with the Lord Jesus himself: *he* is the doctrine; 'I am the truth'. It is not a thing separate from himself. Christ came from heaven, dwells in heaven, abides in the saints, will return from heaven, and shall reign in glory. Oh, what stupendous doctrinal wells: the sight and sound thereof make the saints to shout for joy and sound the high praises of the Lord.

How loved and honoured are the ministers of the gospel, who minister these things unto us: slaves of Jesus Christ, servants with Paul in the gospel, spiritual sons to Paul's evangelical fatherhood, companions of Paul in labour. They are the apostle's true yokefellows, fellowlabourers, fellowsoldiers.

They were so closely connected with him in these bonds: they were not the paid hirelings of the church, or a church; albeit they freely served in the churches. There was no organization: only sweet communion and humble submission to Paul in the gospel. To them there was no society external to the apostle in the ministry. Friend, doth the water flow?

If so, thou shalt experience that of which the apostle wrote. The wells are in a wilderness, and this soon appears in the background of the epistle. Outside of the wells a vista appears as one's gaze sweeps across the barren land: envy, strife, affliction, death, terror, adversity, perdition, conflict, and vainglory.

To the right hand and on the left appears a crooked and perverse nation, before one's face looms the great and terrible day of judgment, and within this vile body groans fluttering a contrite and mortifying spirit of fear and trembling.

Behold! Abasement, sorrow upon sorrow, all seeking their own things in the church, no man likeminded in the ministry.

One is full of heaviness, others are sick nigh unto death. Here is lack, there want and hunger. Around are dogs, evil workers, and the concision. Yonder sounds weeping and weeping again. Nigh draw many enemies of the cross, they mind earthly things, their very glory is their shame, their god their belly.

Mark it, this is the apostolic church of which he speaks. How then is it now so much better, as some blind guides would have us believe? Oh, no! Better only to those who think this worldly wilderness a second paradise.

But to those of us who taste the water from the wells of salvation, the church around brings us tears, sorrow, heaviness, and moreover often gives us contemptuous dismissal and scornful mockery in return for our faithful love and true witness.

But how then can we possibly subsist and endure in such a wilderness? I reply, By drawing water with joy from the wells of salvation. Now observe the refreshment this brings: consolation, comfort, bowels and mercies, love, unity, lowliness, humility, obedience, and faith.

From these waters a spirit of careful rectitude is nourished: the saints have an eye on the day of judgment. They are not *too* secure. They are marked by mortification and soul-watchfulness; one observes their caution, self-judgment, spirituality, earnestness, zeal, humility, and heavenliness.

The church appears. Twenty-two times in corporate terms the saints are mentioned. They are Paul's beloved, sons of God, lights in the world, our beloved brethren, the church. They are Paul's dearly beloved, referred to as both saints and servants. Called the fellowship, they are made partakers of the apostle's grace being his joy and crown. There is a well for the church, you know; Rebekah was found there.

And what divine service appears in that church under such a ministry. One finds the worship, the being found in Christ, the winning Christ, and the knowing him. Withal there is the power of his resurrection, the fellowship of his sufferings, and the being made conformable unto his death.

The word of God sounds abroad. The riches of Christ dwell within. Heavenly conversation strikes the ear. Lowly humility softens the eye. Every heart is melted in the love of God. From each to each flows cherished affection, anxious love, pathetic entreaty. Behold! eternity draws near. Soon the Lord will return from heaven. Their cautioned souls are prepared for that tremendous day; thus prayer and supplication, thanksgiving and praise, give way to the peace that comes from the God of peace, passing all understanding.

Riches in glory, laid up above, already hang trembling upon the air: so near is the world to come. Departing to be with Christ is far, far better than anything remotely conceivable in this fleeting, decaying 'life'. Withal, to the saints, death is no death: it is 'for ever with the Lord'. Amen, so let it be. And there: Lo! there is the book of life. What a well. What a well. Have you looked into it? May God, blessed for evermore, grant that it may be so.

Now unto God and our Father be glory for ever and ever. Amen.

Salute every saint in Christ Jesus. The brethren which are with me greet you.

The grace of our Lord Jesus Christ be with you all. Amen.

John Metcalfe

INDEX

TO OTHER PUBLICATIONS

PSALMS, HYMNS AND SPIRITUAL SONGS

THE PSALMS
OF THE
OLD TESTAMENT

The Psalms of the Old Testament, the result of years of painstaking labour, is an original translation into verse from the Authorised Version, which seeks to present the Psalms in the purest scriptural form possible for singing. Here, for the first time, divine names are rendered as and when they occur in the scripture, the distinction between LORD and Lord has been preserved, and every essential point of doctrine and experience appears with unique perception and fidelity.

The Psalms of the Old Testament is the first part of a trilogy written by John Metcalfe, the second part of which is entitled *Spiritual Songs from the Gospels,* and the last, *The Hymns of the New Testament.* These titles provide unique and accurate metrical versions of passages from the psalms, the gospels and the new testament epistles respectively, and are intended to be used together in the worship of God.

Price £2.50 *(postage extra)*
(hard-case binding, dust-jacket)
Printed, sewn and bound
by the John Metcalfe Publishing Trust
ISBN 0 9506366 7 3

SPIRITUAL SONGS
FROM
THE GOSPELS

The *Spiritual Songs from the Gospels*, the result of years of painstaking labour, is an original translation into verse from the Authorised Version, which seeks to present essential parts of the gospels in the purest scriptural form possible for singing. The careful selection from Matthew, Mark, Luke and John, set forth in metrical verse of the highest integrity, enables the singer to sing 'the word of Christ' as if from the scripture itself, 'richly and in all wisdom'; and, above all, in a way that facilitates worship in song of unprecedented fidelity.

The *Spiritual Songs from the Gospels* is the central part of a trilogy written by John Metcalfe, the first part of which is entitled *The Psalms of the Old Testament*, and the last, *The Hymns of the New Testament*. These titles provide unique and accurate metrical versions of passages from the psalms, the gospels and the new testament epistles respectively, and are intended to be used together in the worship of God.

Price £2.50 *(postage extra)*
(hard-case binding, dust-jacket)
Printed, sewn and bound
by the John Metcalfe Publishing Trust
ISBN 0 9506366 8 1

THE HYMNS
OF THE
NEW TESTAMENT

The *Hymns of the New Testament*, the result of years of painstaking labour, is an original translation into verse from the Authorised Version, which presents essential parts of the new testament epistles in the purest scriptural form possible for singing. The careful selection from the book of Acts to that of Revelation, set forth in metrical verse of the highest integrity, enables the singer to sing 'the word of Christ' as if from the scripture itself, 'richly and in all wisdom'; and, above all, in a way that facilitates worship in song of unprecedented fidelity.

The *Hymns of the New Testament* is the last part of a trilogy written by John Metcalfe, the first part of which is entitled *The Psalms of the Old Testament*, and the next, *Spiritual Songs from the Gospels*. These titles provide unique and accurate metrical versions of passages from the psalms, the gospels and the new testament epistles respectively, and are intended to be used together in the worship of God.

Price £2.50 *(postage extra)*
(hard-case binding, dust-jacket)
Printed, sewn and bound
by the John Metcalfe Publishing Trust
ISBN 0 9506366 9 X

‘THE APOSTOLIC FOUNDATION OF THE CHRISTIAN CHURCH’ SERIES

Third Printing

FOUNDATIONS UNCOVERED

THE APOSTOLIC FOUNDATION
OF THE
CHRISTIAN CHURCH

Volume I

Foundations Uncovered is the introduction to the major series: 'The Apostolic Foundation of the Christian Church'.

Rich in truth, the Introduction deals comprehensively with the foundation of the apostolic faith under the descriptive titles: The Word, The Doctrine, The Truth, The Gospel, The Faith, The New Testament, and The Foundation.

The contents of the book reveal: The Fact of the Foundation; The Foundation Uncovered; What the Foundation is not; How the Foundation is Described; and, Being Built upon the Foundation.

'This book comes with the freshness of a new Reformation.'

Price 75p *(postage extra)*
(Laminated cover)
Printed, sewn and bound
by the John Metcalfe Publishing Trust
ISBN 0 9506366 5 7

Thoroughly revised and extensively rewritten second edition

Third Printing

THE BIRTH OF JESUS CHRIST

THE APOSTOLIC FOUNDATION
OF THE
CHRISTIAN CHURCH

Volume II

'The very spirit of adoration and worship rings through the pages of *The Birth of Jesus Christ.*

'The author expresses with great clarity the truths revealed to him in his study of holy scriptures at depth. We are presented here with a totally lofty view of the Incarnation.

'John Metcalfe is to be classed amongst the foremost expositors of our age; and his writings have about them that quality of timelessness that makes me sure they will one day take their place among the heritage of truly great Christian works.'

From a review by Rev. David Catterson.

'Uncompromisingly faithful to scripture ... has much to offer which is worth serious consideration ... deeply moving.'

The Expository Times.

Price 95p *(postage extra)*
(Laminated Cover)
Printed, sewn and bound
by the John Metcalfe Publishing Trust
ISBN 1 870039 48 3

Thoroughly revised and extensively rewritten second edition (Hardback)

Third Printing

THE MESSIAH

THE APOSTOLIC FOUNDATION
OF THE
CHRISTIAN CHURCH

Volume III

The Messiah is a spiritually penetrating and entirely original exposition of Matthew chapter one to chapter seven from the trenchant pen of John Metcalfe.

Matthew Chapters One to Seven

GENEALOGY · BIRTH · STAR OF BETHLEHEM
HEROD · FLIGHT TO EGYPT · NAZARETH
JOHN THE BAPTIST · THE BAPTIST'S MINISTRY
JESUS' BAPTISM · ALL RIGHTEOUSNESS FULFILLED
HEAVEN OPENED · THE SPIRIT'S DESCENT
THE TEMPTATION OF JESUS IN THE WILDERNESS
JESUS' MANIFESTATION · THE CALLING · THE TRUE DISCIPLES
THE BEATITUDES · THE SERMON ON THE MOUNT

'Something of the fire of the ancient Hebrew prophet .... Metcalfe has spiritual and expository potentials of a high order.'

The Life of Faith.

Price £7.75 *(postage extra)*
Hardback 420 pages
Laminated bookjacket
Printed, sewn and bound
by the John Metcalfe Publishing Trust
ISBN 1 870039 51 3

Second Edition (Hardback)

THE SON OF GOD AND SEED OF DAVID

THE APOSTOLIC FOUNDATION
OF THE
CHRISTIAN CHURCH

Volume IV

The Son of God and Seed of David is the fourth volume in the major work entitled 'The Apostolic Foundation of the Christian Church.'

'The author proceeds to open and allege that Jesus Christ is and ever was *The Son of God.* This greatest of subjects, this most profound of all mysteries, is handled with reverence and with outstanding perception.

'The second part considers *The Seed of David.* What is meant precisely by 'the seed'? And why 'of David'? With prophetic insight the author expounds these essential verities.'

Price £6.95 *(postage extra)*
Hardback 250 pages
Laminated bookjacket
Printed, sewn and bound
by the John Metcalfe Publishing Trust
ISBN 1 870039 16 5

CHRIST CRUCIFIED

THE APOSTOLIC FOUNDATION
OF THE
CHRISTIAN CHURCH

Volume V

Christ Crucified the definitive work on the crucifixion, the blood, and the cross of Jesus Christ.

The crucifixion of Jesus Christ witnessed in the Gospels: the gospel according to Matthew; Mark; Luke; John.

The blood of Jesus Christ declared in the Epistles: the shed blood; the blood of purchase; redemption through his blood; the blood of sprinkling; the blood of the covenant.

The doctrine of the cross revealed in the apostolic foundation of the Christian church: the doctrine of the cross; the cross and the body of sin; the cross and the carnal mind; the cross and the law; the offence of the cross; the cross of our Lord Jesus Christ.

Price £6.95 *(postage extra)*
Hardback 300 pages
Laminated bookjacket
Printed, sewn and bound
by the John Metcalfe Publishing Trust
ISBN 1 870039 08 4

JUSTIFICATION BY FAITH

THE APOSTOLIC FOUNDATION
OF THE
CHRISTIAN CHURCH

Volume VI

THE HEART OF THE GOSPEL · THE FOUNDATION OF THE CHURCH
THE ISSUE OF ETERNITY
CLEARLY, ORIGINALLY AND POWERFULLY OPENED

The basis · The righteousness of the law
The righteousness of God · The atonement · Justification
Traditional views considered · Righteousness imputed to faith
Faith counted for righteousness · Justification by Faith

'And it came to pass, when Jesus had ended these sayings, the people were astonished at his doctrine: for he taught them as one having authority, and not as the scribes.' Matthew 7:28,29.

Price £7.50 *(postage extra)*
Hardback 375 pages
Laminated bookjacket
Printed, sewn and bound
by the John Metcalfe Publishing Trust
ISBN 1870039 11 4

THE CHURCH: WHAT IS IT?

THE APOSTOLIC FOUNDATION
OF THE
CHRISTIAN CHURCH

Volume VII

The answer to this question proceeds first from the lips of Jesus himself, Mt. 16:18, later to be expounded by the words of the apostles whom he sent.

Neither fear of man nor favour from the world remotely affect the answer.

Here is the truth, the whole truth, and nothing but the truth.

The complete originality, the vast range, and the total fearlessness of this book command the attention in a way that is unique.

Read this book: you will never read another like it.

Outspokenly devastating yet devastatingly constructive.

Price £7.75 *(postage extra)*
Hardback 400 pages
Laminated bookjacket
Printed, sewn and bound
by the John Metcalfe Publishing Trust
ISBN 1 870039 23 8

OTHER TITLES

NOAH AND THE FLOOD

Noah and the Flood expounds with vital urgency the man and the message that heralded the end of the old world. The description of the flood itself is vividly realistic. The whole work has an unmistakable ring of authority, and speaks as 'Thus saith the Lord'.

'Mr. Metcalfe makes a skilful use of persuasive eloquence as he challenges the reality of one's profession of faith ... he gives a rousing call to a searching self-examination and evaluation of one's spiritual experience.'

The Monthly Record of the Free Church of Scotland.

Price £1.90 *(postage extra)*
(Laminated Cover)
Printed, sewn and bound
by the John Metcalfe Publishing Trust
ISBN 1 870039 22 X

DIVINE FOOTSTEPS

Divine Footsteps traces the pathway of the feet of the Son of man from the very beginning in the prophetic figures of the true in the old testament through the reality in the new; doing so in a way of experimental spirituality. At the last a glimpse of the coming glory is beheld as his feet are viewed as standing at the latter day upon the earth.

Price 95p *(postage extra)*
(Laminated Cover)
Printed, sewn and bound
by the John Metcalfe Publishing Trust
ISBN 1 870039 21 1

THE RED HEIFER

The Red Heifer was the name given to a sacrifice used by the children of Israel in the Old Testament—as recorded in Numbers 19—in which a heifer was slain and burned. Cedar wood, hyssop and scarlet were cast into the burning, and the ashes were mingled with running water and put in a vessel. It was kept for the children of Israel for a water of separation: it was a purification for sin.

In this unusual book the sacrifice is brought up to date and its relevance to the church today is shown.

Price 75p *(postage extra)*
ISBN 0 9502515 4 2

OF GOD OR MAN?

LIGHT FROM GALATIANS

The Epistle to the Galatians contends for deliverance from the law and from carnal ministry.

The Apostle opens his matter in two ways:

Firstly, Paul vindicates himself and his ministry against those that came not from God above, but from Jerusalem below.

Secondly, he defends the Gospel and evangelical liberty against legal perversions and bondage to the flesh.

Price £1.45 *(postage extra)*
(Laminated Cover)
ISBN 0 9506366 3 0

THE BOOK OF RUTH

The Book of Ruth is set against the farming background of old testament Israel at the time of the Judges, the narrative—unfolding the work of God in redemption—being marked by a series of agricultural events.

These events—the famine; the barley harvest; the wheat harvest; the winnowing—possessed a hidden spiritual significance to that community, but, much more, they speak in figure directly to our own times, as the book reveals.

Equally contemporary appear the characters of Ruth, Naomi, Boaz, and the first kinsman, drawn with spiritual perception greatly to the profit of the reader.

Price £4.95 *(postage extra)*
Hardback 200 pages
Laminated bookjacket
Printed, sewn and bound
by the John Metcalfe Publishing Trust
ISBN 1 870039 17 3

A QUESTION FOR POPE JOHN PAUL II

As a consequence of his many years spent apart in prayer, lonely vigil, and painstaking study of the scripture, John Metcalfe asks a question and looks for an answer from Pope John Paul II.

Price £1.25. *(postage extra)*
(Laminated Cover)
ISBN 0 9506366 4 9

PRESENT-DAY CONVERSIONS
OF THE NEW TESTAMENT KIND

FROM THE MINISTRY OF

JOHN METCALFE

The outstandingly striking presentation of this fascinating paperback will surely catch the eye, as its title and contents will certainly captivate the mind: here is a unique publication.

Woven into a gripping narrative, over twenty-one short life stories, all centred on conversions that simply could not have happened had not God broken in, and had not Christ been revealed, the book presents a tremendous challenge, at once moving and thrilling to the reader.

Price £2.25 *(postage extra)*
(Laminated Cover)
Printed, sewn and bound
by the John Metcalfe Publishing Trust
ISBN 1 870039 31 9

DIVINE MEDITATIONS

OF

WILLIAM HUNTINGTON

Originally published by Mr. Huntington as a series of letters to J. Jenkins, under the title of 'Contemplations on the God of Israel', the spiritual content of this correspondence has been skilfully and sympathetically edited, abridged, and arranged so as to form a series of meditations, suitable for daily readings.

Mr. Huntington's own text is thereby adapted to speak directly to the reader in a way much more suited to his ministering immediately to ourselves, in our own circumstances and times.

It is greatly hoped that many today will benefit from this adaption which carefully retains both the spirit and the letter of the text. If any prefer the original format, this is readily available from several sources and many libraries.

Nevertheless, the publishers believe the much more readable form into which Mr. Huntington's very words have been adapted will appeal to a far wider audience, for whose comfort and consolation this carefully edited work has been published.

Price £2.35 *(postage extra)*
(Laminated Cover)
Printed, sewn and bound
by the John Metcalfe Publishing Trust
ISBN 1 870039 24 6

SAVING FAITH

The sevenfold work of the Holy Ghost in bringing a sinner to saving faith in Christ opened and enlarged.

True faith is the work of God. False faith is the presumption of man. But where is the difference? *Saving Faith* shows the difference.

Price £2.25 *(postage extra)*
Paperback 250 pages
(Laminated Cover)
Printed, sewn and bound
by the John Metcalfe Publishing Trust
ISBN 1 870039 40 8

DELIVERANCE FROM THE LAW
THE WESTMINSTER CONFESSION EXPLODED

Deliverance from the law. A devastating vindication of the gospel of Christ against the traditions of man.

Price £1.90 *(postage extra)*
Paperback 160 pages
(Laminated Cover)
Printed, sewn and bound
by the John Metcalfe Publishing Trust
ISBN 1 870039 41 6

THE BEATITUDES

A unique insight destined to be the classic opening of this wonderful sequence of utterances from the lips of Jesus.

The reader will discover a penetration of the spiritual heights and divine depths of these peerless words in a way ever fresh and always rewarding though read time and time again.

Price £1.90 *(postage extra)*
Paperback 185 pages
(Laminated cover)
Printed, sewn and bound
by the John Metcalfe Publishing Trust
ISBN 1 870039 45 9

COLOSSIANS

This concise and unique revelation of the Epistle to the Colossians has the hallmark of spiritual originality and insight peculiar to the ministry of John Metcalfe. It is as if a diamond, inert and lifeless in itself, has been divinely cut at great cost, so that every way in which it is turned, the light from above is enhanced and magnified to break forth with divine radiance showing colour and depth hitherto unsuspected.

The Trustees give glory and thanks to God for the privilege of producing and subsidising this work.

Price 95p *(postage extra)*
Paperback 135 pages
(Laminated cover)
Printed, sewn and bound
by the John Metcalfe Publishing Trust
ISBN 1 870039 55 6

PHILIPPIANS

The Epistle of Paul the Apostle to the Philippians is opened by this work from the pen of John Metcalfe with that lucid thoroughness which one has come to expect from a ministry received 'not of men, neither by man, but by the revelation of Jesus Christ'.

The work of God at Philippi is traced 'from the first day' until the time at which the epistle was written. Never were Lydia or the Philippian jailor drawn with more lively insight. The epistle itself is revealed in order, with passages—such as 'the mind that was in Christ Jesus'—that evidence the work of no less than a divine for our own times.

The Trustees give glory and thanks to God for the privilege of producing and subsidising this book.

Price £1.90 *(postage extra)*
Paperback 185 pages
(Laminated cover)
Printed, sewn and bound
by the John Metcalfe Publishing Trust
ISBN 1 870039 56 4

MATTHEW

This concise revelation of the essence and structure of the Gospel according to Matthew, the culmination of years of prayer and devotion, retreat and study, opens the mind of the Spirit in the unique vision of Jesus Christ, the son of David, the son of Abraham, recorded in the first gospel.

The Trustees give glory and thanks to God for the privilege of producing and subsidising this work.

Price 95p *(postage extra)*
Paperback 135 pages
(Laminated Cover)
Printed, sewn and bound
by the John Metcalfe Publishing Trust
ISBN 1 870039 61 0

PHILEMON

This penetrating revelation of the epistle to Philemon opens the substance of four consecutive lectures given by John Metcalfe in The Hoare Memorial Hall, Church House, Westminster, London.

The Trustees give glory and thanks to God for the privilege of producing and subsidising this work.

Price £1.90 *(postage extra)*
Paperback 190 pages
(Laminated Cover)
Printed, sewn and bound
by the John Metcalfe Publishing Trust
ISBN 1 870039 66 1

FIRST TIMOTHY

This penetrating revelation of the first epistle to Timothy opens the substance of five consecutive lectures given by John Metcalfe in The Hoare Memorial Hall, Church House, Westminster, London.

The Trustees give glory and thanks to God for the privilege of producing and subsidising this work.

Price £2.00 *(postage extra)*
Paperback 220 pages
(Laminated Cover)
Printed, sewn and bound
by the John Metcalfe Publishing Trust
ISBN 1 870039 67 X

MARK

This penetrating revelation of the gospel according to to Mark opens the substance of seven consecutive lectures given by John Metcalfe in The Hoare Memorial Hall, Church House, Westminster, London.

The Trustees give glory and thanks to God for the privilege of producing and subsidising this work.

Price £2.35 *(postage extra)*
Paperback 290 pages
(Laminated Cover)
Printed, sewn and bound
by the John Metcalfe Publishing Trust
ISBN 1 870039 70 X

NEWLY PUBLISHED

CREATION

This spiritually penetrating and outstandingly original revelation of the Creation opens the substance of five consecutive lectures given by John Metcalfe, commencing in the Hoare Memorial Hall and later moving to the central Assembly Hall, Church House, Westminster, London.

The Trustees give glory and thanks to God for the privilege of producing and subsidising this work.

Price £2.00 *(postage extra)*
Paperback 230 pages
(Laminated Cover)
Printed, sewn and bound
by the John Metcalfe Publishing Trust
ISBN 1 870039 71 8

'TRACT FOR THE TIMES' SERIES

'TRACT FOR THE TIMES' SERIES

The Gospel of God by John Metcalfe. No. 1 in the Series. Laminated Cover, price 25p.

The Strait Gate by John Metcalfe. No. 2 in the Series. Laminated Cover, price 25p.

Eternal Sonship and Taylor Brethren by John Metcalfe. No. 3 in the Series. Laminated Cover, price 25p.

Marks of the New Testament Church by John Metcalfe. No. 4 in the Series. Laminated Cover, price 25p.

The Charismatic Delusion by John Metcalfe. No. 5 in the Series. Laminated Cover, price 25p.

Premillennialism Exposed by John Metcalfe. No. 6 in the Series. Laminated Cover, price 25p.

Justification and Peace by John Metcalfe. No. 7 in the Series. Laminated Cover, price 25p.

Faith or Presumption? by John Metcalfe. No. 8 in the Series. Laminated Cover, price 25p.

The Elect Undeceived by John Metcalfe. No. 9 in the Series. Laminated Cover, price 25p.

Justifying Righteousness by John Metcalfe. No. 10 in the Series. Laminated Cover, price 25p.

Righteousness Imputed by John Metcalfe. No. 11 in the Series. Laminated Cover, price 25p.

The Great Deception by John Metcalfe. No. 12 in the Series. Laminated Cover, price 25p.

A Famine in the Land by John Metcalfe. No. 13 in the Series. Laminated Cover, price 25p.

Blood and Water by John Metcalfe. No. 14 in the Series. Laminated Cover, price 25p.

Women Bishops? by John Metcalfe. No. 15 in the Series. Laminated Cover, price 25p.

The Heavenly Vision by John Metcalfe. No. 16 in the Series. Laminated Cover, price 25p.

EVANGELICAL TRACTS

EVANGELICAL TRACTS

1. **The Two Prayers of Elijah.** Green card cover, price 10p.

2. **Wounded for our Transgressions.** Gold card cover, price 10p.

3. **The Blood of Sprinkling.** Red card cover, price 10p.

4. **The Grace of God that brings Salvation.** Blue card cover, price 10p.

5. **The Name of Jesus.** Rose card cover, price 10p.

6. **The Ministry of the New Testament.** Purple card cover, price 10p.

7. **The Death of the Righteous** (*The closing days of J.B. Stoney*) by A.M.S. (his daughter). Ivory card cover, Price 10p.

8. **Repentance.** Sky blue card cover, price 10p.

9. **Legal Deceivers Exposed.** Crimson card cover, price 10p.

10. **Unconditional Salvation.** Green card cover, price 10p.

11. **Religious Merchandise.** Brown card cover, price 10p.

12. **Comfort.** Pink card cover, price 10p.

13. **Peace.** Grey card cover, price 10p.

14. **Eternal Life.** Cobalt card cover, price 10p.

15. **The Handwriting of Ordinances.** Fawn card cover, price 10p.

16. **'Lord, Lord!'.** Emerald card cover, price 10p.

ECCLESIA TRACTS

ECCLESIA TRACTS

The Beginning of the Ecclesia by John Metcalfe. No. 1 in the Series, Sand grain cover, Price 10p.

Churches and the Church by J.N. Darby. Edited. No. 2 in the Series, Sand grain cover, Price 10p.

The Ministers of Christ by John Metcalfe. No. 3 in the Series, Sand grain cover, Price 10p.

The Inward Witness by George Fox. Edited. No. 4 in the Series, Sand grain cover, Price 10p.

The Notion of a Clergyman by J.N. Darby. Edited. No. 5 in the Series, Sand grain cover, Price 10p.

The Servant of the Lord by William Huntington. Edited and Abridged. No. 6 in the Series, Sand grain cover, Price 10p.

One Spirit by William Kelly. Edited. No. 7 in the Series, Sand grain cover, Price 10p.

The Funeral of Arminianism by William Huntington. Edited and Abridged. No. 8 in the Series, Sand grain cover, Price 10p.

One Body by William Kelly. Edited. No. 9 in the Series, Sand grain cover, Price 10p.

False Churches and True by John Metcalfe. No. 10 in the Series, Sand grain cover, Price 10p.

Separation from Evil by J.N. Darby. Edited. No. 11 in the Series, Sand grain cover, Price 10p.

The Remnant by J.B. Stoney. Edited. No. 12 in the Series, Sand grain cover, Price 10p.

The Arminian Skeleton by William Huntington. Edited and Abridged. No. 13 in the Series, Sand grain cover, Price 10p.

FOUNDATION TRACTS

FOUNDATION TRACTS

1. **Female Priests?** by John Metcalfe. Oatmeal cover, price 25p.

2. **The Bondage of the Will** by Martin Luther. Translated and Abridged. Oatmeal cover, price 25p.

3. **Of the Popish Mass** by John Calvin. Translated and Abridged. Oatmeal cover, price 25p.

4. **The Adversary** by John Metcalfe. Oatmeal cover, price 25p.

5. **The Advance of Popery** by J.C. Philpot. Oatmeal cover, price 25p.

6. **Enemies in the Land** by John Metcalfe. Oatmeal cover, price 25p.

7. **An Admonition Concerning Relics** by John Calvin. Oatmeal cover, price 25p.

8. **John Metcalfe's Testimony Against Falsity in Worship** by John Metcalfe. Oatmeal cover, price 25p.

9. **Brethrenism Exposed** by John Metcalfe. Oatmeal cover, price 25p.

10. **John Metcalfe's Testimony Against The Social Gospel** by John Metcalfe. Oatmeal cover, price 25p.

MINISTRY BY JOHN METCALFE

TAPE MINISTRY BY JOHN METCALFE
FROM ENGLAND AND THE FAR EAST
IS AVAILABLE.

In order to obtain this free recorded ministry, please send your blank cassette (C.90) and the cost of the return postage, including your name and address in block capitals, to the John Metcalfe Publishing Trust, Church Road, Tylers Green, Penn, Bucks, HP10 8LN. Tapelists are available on request.

Owing to the increased demand for the tape ministry, we are unable to supply more than two tapes per order, except in the case of meetings for the hearing of tapes, where a special arrangement can be made.

THE MINISTRY OF THE NEW TESTAMENT

The purpose of this substantial A4 gloss paper magazine is to provide spiritual and experimental ministry with sound doctrine which rightly and prophetically divides the Word of Truth.

Readers of our books will already know the high standards of our publications. They can be confident that these pages will maintain that quality, by giving access to enduring ministry from the past, much of which is derived from sources that are virtually unobtainable today, and publishing a living ministry from the present. Selected articles from the following writers have already been included:

Eli Ashdown · John Berridge · Abraham Booth
John Bradford · John Bunyan · John Burgon
John Calvin · Donald Cargill · John Cennick · J.N. Darby
George Fox · John Foxe · William Gadsby · John Guthrie
William Guthrie · Grey Hazlerigg · William Huntington
William Kelly · John Kennedy · John Kershaw
John Keyt · Hanserd Knollys · John Knox · James Lewis
Martin Luther · Robert Murray McCheyne · John Metcalfe
Thomas Oxenham · Alexander—Sandy—Peden · J.C. Philpot
J.K. Popham · James Renwick · J.B. Stoney · Henry Tanner
Arthur Triggs · John Vinall · John Warburton
John Welwood · George Whitefield · J.A. Wylie

Price £1.75 *(postage included)*
Issued Spring, Summer, Autumn, Winter.

Book Order Form

Please send to the address below:-

		Price	Quantity
A Question for Pope John Paul II		£1.25	......
Of God or Man?		£1.45	......
Noah and the Flood		£1.90	......
Divine Footsteps		£0.95	......
The Red Heifer		£0.75	......
The Wells of Salvation		£2.35	......
The Book of Ruth (Hardback edition)		£4.95	......
Divine Meditations of William Huntington		£2.35	......
Present-Day Conversions of the New Testament Kind		£2.25	......
Saving Faith		£2.25	......
Deliverance from the Law		£1.90	......
The Beatitudes		£1.90	......
Colossians		£0.95	......
Philippians		£1.90	......
Matthew		£0.95	......
Philemon		£1.90	......
First Timothy		£2.00	......
Mark		£2.35	......
Creation		£2.00	......
Psalms, Hymns & Spiritual Songs (Hardback edition)			
The Psalms of the Old Testament		£2.50	......
Spiritual Songs from the Gospels		£2.50	......
The Hymns of the New Testament		£2.50	......
'Apostolic Foundation of the Christian Church' series			
Foundations Uncovered	Vol.I	£0.75	......
The Birth of Jesus Christ	Vol.II	£0.95	......
The Messiah (Hardback edition)	Vol.III	£7.75	......
The Son of God and Seed of David (Hardback edition)	Vol.IV	£6.95	......
Christ Crucified (Hardback edition)	Vol.V	£6.95	......
Justification by Faith (Hardback edition)	Vol.VI	£7.50	......
The Church: What is it? (Hardback edition)	Vol.VII	£7.75	......

Name and Address (in block capitals)

. . . .

. . . .

. . . .

If money is sent with order please allow for postage. Please address to:- The John Metcalfe Publishing Trust, Church Road, Tylers Green, Penn, Bucks, HP10 8LN.

Tract Order Form

Please send to the address below:-

Evangelical Tracts		Price	Quantity
The Two Prayers of Elijah		£0.10	......
Wounded for our Transgressions		£0.10	......
The Blood of Sprinkling		£0.10	......
The Grace of God that Brings Salvation		£0.10	......
The Name of Jesus		£0.10	......
The Ministry of the New Testament		£0.10	......
The Death of the Righteous by A.M.S.		£0.10	......
Repentance		£0.10	......
Legal Deceivers Exposed		£0.10	......
Unconditional Salvation		£0.10	......
Religious Merchandise		£0.10	......
Comfort		£0.10	......
Peace		£0.10	......
Eternal Life		£0.10	......
The Handwriting of Ordinances		£0.10	......
'Lord, Lord!'		£0.10	......
'Tract for the Times' series			
The Gospel of God	No.1	£0.25	......
The Strait Gate	No.2	£0.25	......
Eternal Sonship and Taylor Brethren	No.3	£0.25	......
Marks of the New Testament Church	No.4	£0.25	......
The Charismatic Delusion	No.5	£0.25	......
Premillennialism Exposed	No.6	£0.25	......
Justification and Peace	No.7	£0.25	......
Faith or presumption?	No.8	£0.25	......
The Elect undeceived	No.9	£0.25	......
Justifying Righteousness	No.10	£0.25	......
Righteousness Imputed	No.11	£0.25	......
The Great Deception	No.12	£0.25	......
A Famine in the Land	No.13	£0.25	......
Blood and Water	No.14	£0.25	......
Women Bishops?	No.15	£0.25	......
The Heavenly Vision	No.16	£0.25	......

Name and Address (in block capitals)

....

....

....

If money is sent with order please allow for postage. Please address to:- The John Metcalfe Publishing Trust, Church Road, Tylers Green, Penn, Bucks, HP10 8LN.

Tract Order Form

Please send to the address below:-

		Price	Quantity
Ecclesia Tracts			
The Beginning of the Ecclesia	No.1	£0.10	......
Churches and the Church (J.N.D.)	No.2	£0.10	......
The Ministers of Christ	No.3	£0.10	......
The Inward Witness (G.F.)	No.4	£0.10	......
The Notion of a Clergyman (J.N.D.)	No.5	£0.10	......
The Servant of the Lord (W.H.)	No.6	£0.10	......
One Spirit (W.K.)	No.7	£0.10	......
The Funeral of Arminianism (W.H.)	No.8	£0.10	......
One Body (W.K.)	No.9	£0.10	......
False Churches and True	No.10	£0.10	......
Separation from Evil (J.N.D.)	No.11	£0.10	......
The Remnant (J.B.S.)	No.12	£0.10	......
The Arminian Skeleton (W.H.)	No.13	£0.10	......
Foundation Tracts			
Female Priests?	No.1	£0.25	......
The Bondage of the Will (Martin Luther)	No.2	£0.25	......
Of the Popish Mass (John Calvin)	No.3	£0.25	......
The Adversary	No.4	£0.25	......
The Advance of Popery (J.C. Philpot)	No.5	£0.25	......
Enemies in the Land	No.6	£0.25	......
An Admonition Concerning Relics (John Calvin)	No.7	£0.25	......
John Metcalfe's Testimony Against Falsity in Worship	No.8	£0.25	......
Brethrenism Exposed	No.9	£0.25	......
John Metcalfe's Testimony Against The Social Gospel	No.10	£0.25	......

Name and Address (in block capitals)

....

....

....

If money is sent with order please allow for postage. Please address to:- The John Metcalfe Publishing Trust, Church Road, Tylers Green, Penn, Bucks, HP10 8LN.

Magazine Order Form

Name and Address (in block capitals)

....

....

....

Please send me .... current copy/copies of The Ministry of the New Testament.

Please send me .... year/s subscription.

I enclose a cheque/postal order for £ ....

(Price: including postage, U.K. £1.75; Overseas £1.90)
(One year's subscription: Including postage, U.K. £7.00; Overseas £7.60)

Cheques should be made payable to The John Metcalfe Publishing Trust, and for overseas subscribers should be in pounds sterling drawn on a London Bank.

10 or more copies to one address will qualify for a 10% discount

Back numbers from Spring 1986 available.

Please send to The John Metcalfe Publishing Trust, Church Road, Tylers Green, Penn, Bucks, HP10 8LN

All Publications of the Trust are subsidised by the Publishers.